CLARIFYING JEWISH VALUES

A Handbook of Value Clarification Activities for Group

Leaders, Rabbis, Educators, Teachers, Center Workers,

Camp Counselors and Mental Health Professionals

Dov Peretz Elkins

GROWTH ASSOCIATES
Human Relations Consultants and Publishers
P.O. Box 8429
Rochester, New York 14618
(716) 244-1225

Dr. Dov Peretz Elkins is author and editor of fifteen books on theology,

psychology, and education. He is known throughout North America for his

work as lecturer, educator, workshop leader, human relations consultant,

rabbi, counselor and author.

GROWTH ASSOCIATES
Human Relations Consultants and Publishers
P.O. Box 8429
Rochester, New York 14618
(716) 244-1225

Dedicated to

Sidney B. Simon

and

Howard Kirschenbaum

Facilitators of my own growth

Pioneers in humanistic education

Cherished friends

******

Acknowledgments

The author is deeply indebted to Sidney B. Simon and
Howard Kirschenbaum for introducing him to humanistic education
and value clarification. He also values the training he did under the
guidance of Merrill Harmin at a later date. Simon and Kirschenbaum's
classic handbook, Value Clarification, has been the major source for
this handbook. Acknowledgment is hereby made to their pioneering
efforts and innovative ideas, and thanks to them for encouraging the
adaptation of their work into the field of Jewish education.

****

PREFACE

Dr. Dov Peretz Elkins combines the wisdom of the talmudic scholar with the most modern insights of the humanistic educator. His work joins these two worlds to make a look into what it means to be Jewish a thrilling adventure.

I have the highest respect for what Dov Elkins has done to make Values Clarification theory and practice so incredibly relevant to the search for meaning for Jews of all ages.

Are you ready for an adventure? Dov Elkins has taken some of the most sprightly insights from Values Clarification and woven them into a brilliant fabric, a coat of many colors, to help Jews come to terms with what they truly value.

> Dr. Sidney B. Simon
> Co-author, Values Clarification

******

Dr. Elkins' work is excellent for helping people thoughtfully explore their religious and ethnic values and identity. Its effect is a deepening of participants' Jewish consciousness and commitment; yet this is accomplished with great respect for the individuals' right to set his or her own direction.

> Dr. Howard Kirschenbaum, Director
> National Humanistic Education Center
> Co-author, Values Clarification

****

CONTENTS

Part One

Some of the Theory of Value Clarification

Value Clarification is an exciting methodology which has recently gained the interest and attention of a wide spectrum of general and religious educators. Part of the new trend in "humanistic education", Value Clarification seeks to involve learners in their own education, and to tap the affective, or feeling level, as well as the cognitive aspect of human growth.

Claiming that past approaches to education, including moralizing, laissez-faire and modeling, are inadequate for today's complex, democratic and scientifically advanced society, Value Clarification teaches participants a process through which they can hammer out their own values and attitudes in the face of a constantly changing society.

Value Clarification mentors such as Sidney Simon, Howard Kirschenbaum and Merrill Harmin point to three processes which need development in the process of clarifying personal values: choosing, prizing, acting. Each strategy in this handbook involves one or more of these goals: (1) to help learners choose more carefully from among the many alternatives facing them in today's Jewish world: (2) to state clearly and publicly the positions they advocate and the reasons behind them; and (3) to select appropriate actions and deeds to implement the values selected and declared.

Value Clarification is based on John Dewey's philosophy of education which states that persons learn most from their own experience rather than from listening to the experience of others (lectures, books). This viewpoint in no way contradicts the important emphasis placed in Jewish tradition upon intellectual pursuits and the high priority given to book knowledge. It merely carries such learning to the next logical conclusion, already adumbrated in Jewish literature (particularly and most recently in Hasidic literature) that a person with knowledge but without deeds is like a donkey carrying a cargo of heavy books on his back. The experiential method of learning, using affective methods and the inter-active learning process, is more likely to help learners turn cognitive learning into personal experience and accepted values. In a total program of Jewish education, reading and lectures should be accompanied by experiential activities, such as Value Clarification, to enable them more directly to apply to the personal lives of the learners.

One more word. While Value Clarification strategies provide an enjoyable and engaging learning atmosphere, these strategies should not be looked upon merely as "fun and games." A trained teacher, facilitator or group worker should be present to guide the group using these experiences in the most constructive channels, and to maximize the educational effectiveness, as well as to avoid possible pitfalls and problems.

******

Why I Love Value Clarification

I love Value Clarification because it is <u>experiential</u>.

I learned Value Clarification from Howard Kirschenbaum and Sidney B. Simon. Sid Simon learned it (and adapted and added to it) from Louis Raths. And Louis Raths developed it from the theories of John Dewey, master educator and philosopher. Dewey, in <u>Education and Experience</u> (N.Y.: Macmillan, 1959), stresses the importance of learning from quality experiences.

When I listen to a lecture or read a book, I am hearing <u>about someone else's experience</u>. If I participate in an activity, exercise, or project, then examine what happened <u>to me</u> during that experience, I not only learn from that experience, but I also am learning <u>how to learn from</u> my experience. To me one of the most significant things to learn in the educational process is how to examine my life and what happens to me so that I can use that experience, process it, and be different after that experience.

Thus, I love Value Clarification because in addition to reading about and listening to others relate their experiences, I have a method through which I can learn from <u>my own</u> experience.

Secondly, I love Value Clarification because through its methods I as an educator can be <u>facilitative</u> of another's growth without robbing the learning of his autonomy.

If I tell my students what to think, how to act, and what to feel, I am infantilizing them, not teaching them. I want to help them facilitate their own learning. After over twenty years in the classroom, (as well as acting as educator, administrator, youth adviser, supervisor, teacher trainer and educational ideologist), I have come to the firm conclusion that I can't <u>teach any-body anything</u>! I can only help them teach themselves.

Thus, when I get "preachy" and moralize, and insist that I have the right viewpoint, and the right values, I not only am not an effective educator from a tactical point of view, but I am also shrinking my students' capacity to make judgments and be autonomous, and thus instead of helping them to grow and mature, am keeping them dependent and juvenile.

Published originally in <u>Alternatives in Religious</u> Education, Fall, 1977. Reprinted by permission.

This, I believe, is the answer to those opponents of Value Clarification who say that this methodology is O.K. for secular schools, but not for a Jewish school which has a specific set of values to teach and inculcate. If I truly want to transmit traditional Jewish values, I do it best if I present the traditional material and its value system, and then I help the student examine it critically and develop a process through which he can assimilate that which seems to fit his own unique organism best.

In teacher training workshops I am frequently asked, "Yes, but suppose the child then, after having learned a process to create his/her own values, decides to think and believe and do things which are contrary to Jewish tradition?"

My standard answer to that question is: That option is available to students within any educational methodology. If I present Jewish values as the "correct" values, they may still reject them, and decide to think and believe and do things contrary to Jewish tradition. In fact, the more authoritarian I am, the more fundamentalist I appear as a teacher, the more likely my students will be to reject the ideas I am trying to present.

It has been paradoxical to me that when I present Value Clarification to teachers from very traditional schools, they most often become extremely enthusiastic and excited about these approaches. They see Value Clarification as a way to enable their students to become excited and involved in the learning process and they have the confidence that when put to the test, their students will make good decisions. The occasional rebels and nay-sayers are usually the super-liberals who feel that if tender young learners are left "on their own," we have not discharged our obligation to the ideal of Jewish survival.

I don't want to appear to be moralizing or authoritarian in presenting my views of Value Clarification. I want to make it clear that what I am writing is my personal viewpoint and flows from my own experience. Others have the right to accept or reject my views and the methods I describe and use. What I would like, however, is that if people reject the use of Value Clarification, that it be out of sound and carefully examined thought and reflection. To deny the value of this methodology because it leaves too much freedom to the learner is not a sound position in my view. All teaching methods ultimately leave decision-making and value-creating to the learner. There is no way, short of torture (which would last only as long as the pain continues), to coerce a person to accept the values of another. Once we assume the ultimate autonomy of the learner, the most educationally effective way to assure ourselves of reasonable success in transmitting values, is to teach students (or help them learn, more precisely) a process through which they can establish their own values, and test traditional values against their own needs and experiences.

Thirdly, I love Value Clarification because it deals with the <u>affective</u> <u>dimension</u> of persons as well as the cognitive. Value Clarification is holistic, integrated, and multi-dimensional. For too long we have been seeing people as physical shells with a brain and no heart. As a Conservative Rabbi and as a committed Jew, I want to help mold a "hartzliche Yid," not a "hamor nosay sefarim." It is not enough for me to have my students memorize verses and study historical dates and analyze the causes of Jewish migrations.

I want my students to learn the joy of Jewish living, to celebrate the rites of passage in their own lives and in the corporate life of the Jewish people with ecstasy and enthusiasm. I want them to be afraid for the survival of our people, and quiver and quake, and maybe even have a few nightmares over the suffering of Syrian and Soviet Jewry, I want them to scream, and rage and march, when Israel is threatened. And I want them to shout in indignation when human beings of any faith, race or creed are diminished in any way, or denied their freedom, or treated unjustly. Values Clarification has presented, for me, a way to help students get in touch with these deep feelings about Judaism, the Jewish People, the world, and the fate of humankind.

Fourthly, I love Value Clarification because it involves the Interactive Learning Process (I. L. P.). Values strategies often involve the breakdown of a large group into smaller groups of twos, three, fours, and fives. In this way students learn from each other, have more opportunities to express themselves and articulate their viewpoints, attitudes and feelings, and thus learn much more than by passive listening. Equally important is the fact that participants in values strategies get to know one another, often very intimately, and begin to feel like a <u>community</u> and not just an <u>audience</u>.

In most Jewish classrooms students come from several different neighborhoods and may not attend the same public schools. Value Clarification strategies help groups of people overcome the communication barriers, and begin to encourage self-disclosure and personal sharing of their lives as well as their ideas, ideals and hopes. People learn better in this environment because there is trust and warmth and caring. They begin to see Jewish education and the Jewish school as a loving place, a nourishing place, and not an extra burden; something to look forward to instead of something to dread.

Fifthly, I love Value Clarification because it is humanistic. As I pointed out in my book, <u>Humanizing Jewish Life: Judaism, and the Human Potential</u> <u>Movement</u> (A. S. Barnes, 1976), the term humanistic for me means <u>person-centered</u>.

Learning and growth must meet the needs of the individual. People learn what they need to learn, not what we want them to learn. Thus, Jewish education cannot be text-centered, or school-centered or tradition-centered. It must be person-centered, in my view, if it is to be effective.

Jewish education must deal with the things that make a difference in the personal lives of the students. Value Clarification strategies help me as a learning facilitator to reach the key issues of the students' lives. This methodology has enough flexibility and enough dynamism to permit the learning community to carry the ball to the ultimate and important issues. It focuses on what is important to the students. That is the only kind of learning that will stick to the bones. Students will learn not what I as a rabbi and educator and teacher want them to remember in order to help Jewish people survive. Rather they will learn what will be useful to them as persons, as human beings, to grow and develop.

I love Judaism enough and respect and admire it enough to have the confidence and faith that students will find within Judaism an abundance of ideals, values, and attitudes to make their personal lives fuller, richer, more meaningful and more satisfying. Those are the things people are looking for. Commitment to the State of Israel, to Jewish learning, to Klal Yisrael, to ethical living, to participation in Jewish community life, to prayer, to mitzvot, will all come to the life of a student who finds Judaism meaningful and enriching to his personal life, as I have found it. Such commitments and loyalties to things Jewish will not come because teachers and principals and school boards want to preserve Judaism or want the Jewish people to survive. Those values will become important to young people only if they see in them some direct connection to their personal fulfillment, and to the fulfillment of their organismic needs for meaning, compassion, integration, altruism, love and service.

In sum, I love Value Clarification because I have found it to be one of the most effective ways I know to realize the rabbinic ideal (Gen. R. 44:1) - that the ultimate purpose of the mitzvot (the Jewish way of life) is to purify, enrich and enhance the quality of human life.

******

Guidelines for the Leader

To maximize the effectiveness of using Value Clarification activities, the following guidelines can be used:

1) Create an accepting atmosphere.

It is important that a warm, caring and accepting environment be created for participants to be able to express themselves fully and openly. There is no single right answer to most of the complex issues facing persons and Jewish communities today. The Talmud recognized this long ago when it declared that "both these and these are the words of the living God." Disagreement, argumentation, conflict, are all prized in Talmudic dialectic, rather than frowned upon or looked upon as something evil. Nowhere in Talmudic literature is anyone called a fool or miscreant for holding unpopular views. The sages even went so far as to study from Elisha ben Abuya whose theological beliefs were diametrically opposed to the major of the scholars. They did not agree with him, but they also did not deny themselves the opportunity of listening to his wisdom and learning from him.

When personal opinions are shared in values activities, the leader can respond by saying "Thank you," or "O.K.", rather than "good," or "Oh, I like that idea," which seems to give approval or disapproval. After others' opinions are expressed, the leader should express his too. Being a leader does not deny him the privilege of holding his own viewpoint. It can be completely divergent from that of others, in the spirit of "both these and these are the words of the living God."

By respecting the right of each individual to hold his own viewpoint, the leader is acting in accordance with the most effective pedagogical principles of facilitating human growth and learning rather than forcing conformity through authoritarian methods. And at the same time the leader is acting in accordance with the highest ethical standards of Jewish tradition which accords each individual, created in the image of God, the right to have his own thoughts, feelings and beliefs.

I have a great faith and trust in the Jewish way of life that exposure to its riches in an open and accepting atmosphere will ultimately lead the individual, by his own decision and valuing process, to a love, respect and commitment to the heritage of his ancestors.

2) Be a full participant

As others in the group are making an inventory of 20 favorite Jewish activities, or writing a self contract, or composing a letter to the editor or an "I urge" telegram, the leader should be doing so right along with them.

The process of hammering out values is a life-long endeavor, and one is never able to say he has arrived. "It is not your duty to finish the work, but neither are you free to desist from it." (Pirke Avot). The search for Jewish values starts at birth and ends at the grave.

3) Establish the right to pass

The greatness of the Value Clarification approach to learning is that it personalizes the learning process. Learners get beyond the facts and concepts level, and reach into the deep recesses of the soul, the level of personal values, hopes, beliefs, experiences. It is unfair, insensitive and unethical to push a person too hard into those dark unknown places. He will go there when ready. The leader must never rob the learner of his educational autonomy. Education must never become cultural imperialism. The leader should remind the group again and again that they need not say anything, do anything, or participate in anything that is threatening, uncomfortable or scary. They may choose to risk themselves or push themselves, and say and do new things, and stretch their own spiritual, emotional and Jewish beings. But it is their own decision when they are ready to do that. A warm, accepting, encouraging, atmosphere will help them achieve the readiness to take the risks toward openness and growth which brings real and long-lasting learning.

4) The rule of unfinished business

Values are always in process. No activity will ever help a person reach "the final truth." Many times participants will be caught in the middle of an important thought or issue, when the group at large is ready to move forward. Sometimes it is possible for the group to pause and help an individual work through an issue. Sometimes, often in fact, many individuals will have to put their discussion on "hold" and return to it during a break, after the session, or in private time. Participants should be told and reminded that unfinished business is natural, normal and common in values discussions, and should come to accept it as part of their on-going search for a life of values.

5) The leader must be committed to the valuing process

The leader must himself be commiting to the process of evolutionary living, always changing, growing and stretching his whole being. This involves study, workshops, in-service training, familiarization with other newer methods in humanistic education, and may also include workshops in personal growth, creativity, awareness, communication skills, and other areas of human relations training.

Being a Jew means being the best kind of human being one can be, and utilizing every possible available resource to achieve that. "The mitzvot (laws) were given to refine humankind." (Talmud) The ultimate quest of the Jewish way of life is make human beings fuller, richer, more fully functioning, more self-actualized, more emotionally, spiritually and intellectually mature with each passing day.

It is the author's deep hope and belief that the use of Value Clarification and other related methodologies in humanistic education and human relations training, through this Handbook and its companion, <u>Jewish Consciousness Raising</u>, will enlarge and enrich the way of Torah in the twentieth century.

******

Note on the use of personal pronouns:

One of the writer's values is to encourage sexual equality and to avoid sexist references. For lack of a better system, he apologizes for usage of he/his/him. He finds use of he/she, him/her, his/hers awkward, and asks the reader to mentally supply this meaning at all times when he, him, or his is used.

******

Some Further Resources

I   Books on Value Clarification

Values Clarification - A Handbook of Strategies
    Sidney Simon, Howard Kirschenbaum, Leland Howe $5.25

A Reader in Values Clarification ed. Howard Kirschenbaum
    and Sidney Simon $6.25

Personalizing Education by Leland Howe and Mary Martha Howe $6.

A Practical Guide to Value Clarification by Maury Smith $10.50

Advanced Value Clarification by Howard Kirschenbaum $9.00

II Books on Humanistic Education

Humanistic Education Sourcebook ed. Don Read & Sidney Simon $8.2

Will the Real Teacher Please Stand Up? A Primer in Humanistic
    Education. Ed. Mary Greer & Bonnie Rubinstein $8.25

Freedom to Learn by Carl R. Rogers $5.75

The above books can be ordered from:

        National Humanistic Education Center
        110 Spring Street
        Saratoga Springs, N.Y. 12866

(Postage is included in prices above. Canadian orders add 5%
    for additional postage. Non-tax-exempt New York State
    residents add 6% sales tax. Send orders WITH PAYMENT.)

*****

Educational Materials
by Dr. Dov Peretz Elkins

Humanizing Jewish Life: Judaism & the Human Potential Movement (A.S. Barnes, 1976) $11

Glad To Be Me: Building Self-Esteem in Yourself & Others (Prentice-Hall, Spectrum Books, paperback, 1976) $5 (Second printing, April 1977)

Teaching People to Love Themselves - A Leader's Handbook of Theory and Technique for Self-Esteem & Affirmation Training. 325 pp. (Growth Associates, 1977) $16

Clarifying Jewish Values: Values Activities for Jewish Groups (Growth Associates, 1977) $10

Jewish Consciousness Raising. A Handbook of 50 experiential exercises and activities for Jewish groups. (Growth Associates, 1977) $10

Meeting Your Jewish Self: Personal Growth for Jews (Spring 1978) Tentative: $7

Self Concept Sourcebook (Prentice-Hall, Spectrum Books, 1978) Tentative: $7

Shepherd of Jerusalem: A Biography of Chief Rabbi Abraham Isaac Kook (Shengold, 1976) $6.50

A Tradition Reborn: Sermons & Essays on Liberal Judaism (A.S. Barnes, 1973) $2

God's Warriors: Dramatic Adventures of Rabbis in Uniform (Jonathan David, 1974) $2

Treasures from the Dust: Discoveries in Biblical Archeology with Azriel Eisenberg (Abelard-Schuman, 1972) $2

Worlds Lost and Found: Discoveries in Biblical Archeology with Azriel Eisenberg; winner of Jewish Book Council Prize (Abelard-Schuman, 1964). Out of print, available in libraries. May be reprinted in 1978 - write for information if interested.

Rejoice with Jerusalem: Prayers, Readings & Songs for Israel Observances (Prayer Book Press, 1972, 50 pages, paperback) $2.50

The Tallit: Some Modern Meanings (Jewish Tract Series, Burning Bush Press, 30 pages, 1976) $1

Proud To Be Me: Raising Self-Esteem in Individuals, Families, Schools & Minority Groups (An earlier version of **Glad To Be Me** including a major section on Jewish self-esteem omitted from **Glad To Be Me**. Note that **Glad To Be Me** also contains much material not found in **Proud To Be Me**.) (Growth Associates, 1975) $6.50

So Young to be a Rabbi: The Education of an American Clergyman (Yoseloff, 1969) $2

☐ Please send me the books checked above.

☐ I enclose $2 for a packet of Dr. Elkins' most recent journal and magazine articles on the theory & programs of Judaism and the Human Potential Movement (written after **Humanizing Jewish Life**), from such periodicals as "Alternatives," "A.H.P. Monthly," "Pastoral Services," and others.

☐ Check here if interested in information on lectures, workshops and/or other training events.

NAME _____

ORGANIZATIONAL AFFILIATION_____ POSITION _____

ADDRESS _____

CITY _____ STATE _____ ZIP _____

TELEPHONE _____

Send orders **WITH PAYMENT** to: Growth Associates
Human Relations Consultants
P.O. Box 8429
Rochester, NY 14618
(716) 244-1225

N.Y. State residents add 7% sales tax, please.

Twenty Jewish Activities I Enjoy Most

Goal

What areas of Jewish life, Jewish community, Jewish religion, Jewish culture, are most significant to me? Most Jews have pride in their heritage and are proud to be associated with the Jewish people. This identification with the Jewish People and Judaism takes many forms, depending on the individual. Rabbis, social scientists and active lay leaders of the Jewish community share a general feeling that despite the pride and contentment Jews have in their tradition and people, they rarely act upon these feelings in a significant way. In order to help us clarify what are the Jewish activities, involvements, commitments, which we enjoy most and from which we derive most satisfaction, we have to examine them and reflect on them. What parts of Jewishness do we value most? This can be determined by trying to recall those activities which we enjoy doing most. This exercise in listing twenty favorite Jewish activities will help us to examine our most prized and cherished Jewish activities.

Instructions:

On the pages following, in the places designated, list the twenty Jewish activities which you enjoy doing most. They can be big or small things, important or simple, things which you have done often or rarely (and would like to do more). Define "enjoy" any way you want. Remember that this exercise is very subjective, and only you know what you like. Don't rely on any outside standards or on any other person's feelings.

Not everyone will be able to find exactly twenty; others may find less. The number twenty is approximate. Find as many as you can in the time allotted. To help you think of more, let your mind reflect on your entire life, then perhaps on the last year; think of the different seasons of the year, of different stages of life; of different places you have been; of different ages of your life; of the members of your family, congregation, community, who might have shared these activities with you.

Example: Jewish activities I like best are: Singing Hatikva in a large group of thousands of Jews; chanting kedusha at Shabbat morning musaf services; watching a bride and groom march down the aisle of a synagogue on the way to a Huppah.

Now write your favorite Jewish activities below: (Ignore the six narrow columns to the left until later.)

MY FAVORITE JEWISH ACTIVITIES

$	I or C	R or C	N5	1-5	Date	#	
						1	
						2	
						3	
						4	
						5	
						6	
						7	
						8	
						9	
						10	
						11	
						12	

$	I or C	R or C	N 5	1-5	Date	#	
						13	
						14	
						15	
						16	
						17	
						18	
						19	
						20	

Coding:

The following instructions will explain the six columns to the left of each activity you listed.

1) In the first column to the far left, make a dollar sign ($) next to any activity which costs more than $3 each time it is done.

2) In the second column write the letter "I" next to each activity which you prefer to do as an individual. Write the letter "C" next to each activity you prefer to do as a Community or in any kind of group setting. Write both "I" and "C" if you enjoy doing the activity equally as an individual or as a community.

3) In the third column write the letter "R" next to those activities which are normally considered Religious. Write the letter "C" next to activities which are more ethnically, or Culturally Jewish. Write both "R" and "C" if the activity fits into both categories equally.

4) In the fourth column enter the code N5 next to the Jewish activities which would not have been listed by you five years ago.

5) Rank order your five favorite activities on this list. Place a "1" next to your favorite activity, "2" next to your next favorite, etc.

6) Write the date you last engaged in that activity.

Follow-up Things To Do

Following is a list of ways to utilize what you have written in your activity book that help you learn more about yourself and your Jewish feelings, attitudes and commitments. Do as many as you are interested in and have time for. It is important that no one be pressured into saying or sharing anything publicly which he does not want to.

(1) Form groups of four people. Let each person take three minutes to describe how he likes to do the activity he marked with the number one in the rank-order column (column 5 from left). Describe the ideal conditions under which you might like to do that activity next time. If you prefer, you may wish to talk about the activity you listed as second or third. (Example: with whom, at what time, under what circumstances, etc.)

(2) Form groups of two or three people. You might break your previous group of four into two groups of two. Choose one of the five items you listed as having highest priority and discuss three advantages, joys, benefits, nachas, you derive from that activity. Let each person take three minutes.

(3) In the entire group - or in groups of 20 to 25 if the group is larger - discuss some of the following questions:

    a) What did I learn from the money column?
       (Examples: "I learned that it's expensive to be a
               good Jew"; "I learned that most of
               the things I enjoy are free.")

b) Which received more codes in your second column, activities which you like to do as an individual, or as a community?

c) How did people define "religious" and "cultural" and and which activities are more popular? Did the group share common definitions? "I learned about myself that....."

d) Some conclusions we might draw about the Jewish community are...
Some conclusions we might draw about our group are...
Some conclusions I might draw about myself are...

(4) In groups of three, let each person share with the others in his small tryad some decisions, actions, prioritizing of schedule which he has to do in his life. (Examples: I have to set aside an hour a day to read the Bible; I have to get home more often for Friday night dinner; I have to travel to Israel more often, etc.,etc., etc.)

(5) Share any other learnings as yet unexpressed by you with the entire group. Make these in the form of I learned..." statements. Other kinds of statements might be:

"I re-learned that..."
"I noticed that..."
"I discovered that..."
"I was surprised that..."
"I was pleased that..."
"I was displeased that..."
"I think our community should..."
"I think our organization has to..."
"From now on..."
"Some things I need to do are..."

(6) Make a Jewish Values Diary

On the lines following, list five to ten of the most important things you learned about yourself, your life, your Jewish activities, your commitments, your priorities, your needs, your loves, your fears, etc., etc. Take ten to fifteen minutes to do this individually.

1) _____
2) _____
3) _____
4) _____
5) _____
6) _____
7) _____
8) _____
9) _____
10) _____

If you want, you might share some of these with the group.

(7)   Make a self-contract

        Form dyads (groups of two). Let each partner select one of
the ten items written on the above list for concentrated attention.
Make a pledge or promise to yourself (like a "New Years' Resolution")
that you will stop something, or begin something, or change something
in your Jewish life. Make it realistic, specific and achievable. Take
a few minutes to think about a meaningful forward step for your own
Jewish self-development and growth.

        For example: I will kiss the mezuzah every time I leave the
house; I will visit the Jewish Old Age Home once every two months;
I will find a pen-pal in Israel and write at least six letters to him in
the next year.

        Let the other member of your dyad sign your self-contract as
a witness.

Self-Contract of_____

I promise myself that_____

_____

_____

Check-up date _____

Signed _____

Witness_____

(8)   My dyad partner is

His promise, contract, to himself, is

_____

_____

_____

_____

Date I should check and remind him about his self-contract
is: _____

Enter this information into your personal calendar to remind your
partner. Enter your own self-contract to remind yourself, and
know when to expect a reminder-call from your partner about your
own self-contract.

******

Some thoughts I have now are

_____

_____

_____

_____

_____

Some feelings I have now are

_____

_____

_____

_____

_____

******

Jewish Values Grid

Goal

The purpose of the Jewish Values Grid is to examine the values of the participants in terms of the seven valuing processes set out by Louis Raths in Values and Teaching (Columbus, Ohio: Charles E. Merrill, 1966) Others who have used this exercise have found that their values need strengthening and clarification, since often they do not meet all seven of Rath's criteria for a true value.

The Valuing Process

According to Louis Raths, what most people consider values are really only value indicators, or things which may be on the way to becoming a value. This is the case because the value indicators do not fulfill all seven processes of becoming a full-fledged value. For example, a person may say that he values Jewish education, but he himself does not read or study about Judaism, he does not support any institutions of Jewish learning, and he is not active in any organization that furthers Jewish education. He may think Jewish education is important, but it is not, according to Raths' definition, a real value. It is only a value indicator--something which may become a real value for him some day.

These are the seven valuing processes (for further discussion, see Values and Teaching, Chapter 3, "Values and Valuing"):

1) Choosing freely, with no coercion or pressure
2) Choosing from alternatives
3) Choosing reflectively - considering the consequences
4) Prizing and cherishing - feeling proud about the value
5) Publicly affirming the value - willingness to tell others openly and freely
6) Acting on our choices - doing something concrete about the value
7) Acting often - doing something repetitively about our values

Instructions:

Below you will find a "values grid." In the first column are fourteen Jewish issues (not in any special order). In the second column write a brief statement about your own personal position on that issue. Only a few key words are necessary. The seven boxes following each issue refer to the seven processes in valuing. Place a check next to the issue if that particular step in the valuing process applies to your position on that issue. If any step does not apply, leave the box blank.

For example, the first issue is the importance of the State of Israel in your life. My position on that issue would be as follows: passionately committed to Israel's creative survival. In box #1, I would place a check, since I chose that position freely. My alternatives: to be a Zionist, anti-Zionist, or non-Zionist (apathetic). Box #2 would thus receive a check ("choosing from alternatives"). Since I considered the consequences of my choice, in terms of my choice, in terms of my charity giving, the organization I join, the books I read, etc., etc., I chose this position reflectively, giving thoughtful consideration to all the pros and cons of my stand on Israel. I would thus check box #3. Continue the steps through step #7 - ("acting repetitively").

Alternative Activity:

Instead of, or in addition to, this activity, you might take a sheet of paper and list ten or fifteen different issues in Jewish life which you might like to test against the seven valuing processes. Another possibility is to combine both approaches by using the fourteen listed, and add five more of your own.

Whichever way you choose, proceed now to write down your stands on the issues written on the left column (or ones you've decided upon) and check (or leave blank) the seven boxes on the right of the issue.

VALUES GRID

	ISSUE	YOUR POSITION	1	2	3	4	5	6	7
1	State of Israel								
2	Shabbat Observance								
3	The Hebrew Language								
4	Unity of the Jewish people								
5	Compassion toward all living things								
6	Intermarriage								
7	Passion for learning								
8	Prayer								
9	Zedaka (charity)								
10	Social Justice								
11	Family Unity								
12	Belief in God								
13	Resistance to persecution								
14	Brotherhood of all people								
15	(add your own list below)								
16									
17									
18									
19									
20									

Follow-up Things To Do

(1)   Form groups of three (tryads), with each person talking about five minutes to discuss one of the issues, his position on it, and how it met, or didn't meet, the seven valuing processes.

        The focus of discussion is not on the content of your beliefs, but rather on the processes with which you have arrived at them, or more importantly, how firm your belief is. Is it a true value, or how close to a value is it?

(2)   Return to the larger group, and let volunteers tell which value or belief they selected, state their position briefly, and how many of the seven processes it fulfilled.

(3)   Were there any patterns in the group's beliefs/values? What did you learn from sharing in the group the various reactions to this values clarification experience?

(4)   Members of the group can now try to make some generalizations about Jewish values which flowed from the processes and activities that took place up to this point. Such statements can begin with "I learned...", "I discovered...", "I was surprised that..." etc., etc.

(5)   Let each individual write in this workbook some steps he would like to take to intensify beliefs and attitudes and value indicators to bring them closer to real values. Pick three beliefs, either from the list suggested, or from your own list, or both, which you would like to strengthen and work on during the next month or two, and state what ways you can strengthen these convictions to make them closer to true values. Do this now on the next page.

STEPS I WANT TO TAKE TO STRENGTHEN MY JEWISH VALUES:

	ISSUE	WHAT I'D LIKE TO DO ABOUT MY CONVICTIONS
1		
2		
3		

(6)   Volunteers may now share what steps they have to take in their own lives to strengthen their convictions.

(7)   What can the Jewish community as a whole, or your group or organization, do to help Jews become more aware of some important Jewish values, and to carry them out in their lives?

******

Percentage Questions

Goal

The purpose of this exercise is to encourage participants to give careful thought to their own ways of thinking and acting. Many of the important issues in Jewish community life, and in one's own personal Jewish life, are never examined with our personal microscope. Putting numerical values on some significant either-or questions will go a long way in helping a person to establish conscious priorities for the major Jewish issues in his life.

Instructions

In each item on the list below you will be asked to write two percentage figures. Naturally, the two together must add up to 100%. Being forced to put numerical values on your beliefs, attitudes, values, and actions will help you to know where you stand, and what changes you might want to make in your life. Even if it seems uncomfortable, and even if you feel "forced" to make these choices, go along with the exercise and see how you react after you have completed it. Experience shows that while it may seem somewhat artificial to begin with, it does help to clarify where we stand in our Jewish lives.

For example, what percentage of your income (allowance, if you are a young person) is spent, and what percentage saved? The answer might be: 70% spent, 30% saved; or 50% spent, 50% saved; or 98% spent, 2% saved. Remember, there is no "right answer." No one will be judged for his answers. The activity is merely a guide and a goal to help you realize what ways you think and act, so that you can examine your thoughts and actions, and be better able to make changes in your life where you want to.

Percentage Question Chart

"What Percentage" Question	%	%
(1) What percentage of your close friends (define "close" any way you feel comfortable) are Jewish, and what percentage not.	Jewish %	non-Jewish %
(2) What percentage of the books you read are Jewish? Other?	Jewish books %	Other %
(3) What percentage of your time is used for Jewish activities? Other activities	Jewish activ. %	Other %

		Charity %	Other %
(4)	What percentage of your income do you use for charity? For other things?		

		Jewish Charity %	Other %
(5)	What percentage of the charity you give goes to specifically Jewish causes?		

		Israel %	US needs %
(6)	What percentage of your contributions to the Jewish Community Federation should go to Israel? What percentage to U.S. Jewish needs.		

		National %	Local %
(7)	What percentage of that which goes to U.S. Jewish needs should go to national organizations, and what % to local needs?		

		Jewish education %	Other %
(8)	What percentage of that which is given to local needs should go to Jewish education, and what % to other causes?		

		Hebrew %	Other %
(9)	What percentage of time spent in religious education should go to Hebrew language and what percentage to other subjects, taught in English, such as history, ethics, customs literature, etc.?		

		Jewish studies %	secular %
(10)	What percentage of one's educational time should be spent in secular studies and what % in Jewish Studies? (Include classroom and any other time spent on learning.)		

		Traditional %	Modern %
(11)	What percentage of public Jewish worship should be spent in using traditional prayers (in Hebrew or English)? Modern prayers?		

		Hebrew %	English %
(12)	What percentage of public Jewish prayer should should be in Hebrew and what % in English?		

		Prayer & Study %	Other %
(13)	What percentage of your life is spent in prayer and Jewish study and what % in other areas?		

		Jewish %	American %
(14)	What percentage of you is "American" and what percentage is "Jewish"? (A "toughy" but try it anyway.)		

		Universalist %	Particularist %
(15)	What percentage of you is "universalist" and what % "particularist"?		

		Happy	Unhappy
(16)	What percentage of you is happy with being Jewish, and what percentage unhappy or uncomfortable?	%	%

		Jewish	Non-Jewish
(17)	What percentage of your married friends are married to Jewish spouses? Non-Jewish?	%	%

		Jewish	Non-Jewish
(18)	What percentage of your dates are Jewish? Non-Jewish?	%	%

		Lobbying	Other
(19)	What percentage of your time is spent lobbying for Israel? Other matters?	%	%

		Keep Shabbat	Not Keep
(20)	What percentage of traditional Jewish laws regarding Shabbat do you keep? Not keep?	%	%

		Attend	Not Attend
(21)	What percentage of the time do you attend Shabbat services? Not attend?	%	%

		Tradition	Own Decision
(22)	What percentage of your life should be lived in accordance with Jewish tradition and what percentage in accordance with your own decisions?	%	%

		Nice, Warm	Not...
(23)	What percentage of the rabbis you know are nice, warm people? Not nice, warm people?	%	%

		Warm friendly	Not....
(24)	What percentages of the synagogues you are familiar with are warm, friendly, fun places? Not warm, friendly, fun places?	%	%

		Women	Men
(25)	What percentage of the aliyot (Thorah honors) on Shabbat morning should be given to women? To men?	%	%

		Jews	Non-Jew
(26)	What percentage of Jews should we have in the U.S. Congress? Non-Jews?	%	%

		Jewish	Non-Jewish
(27)	What percentage of the population in America should be Jewish? Non-Jewish?	%	%

		Jewish	Non-Jewish
(28)	What percentage of Jews should we have on the Supreme Court of the U.S.? Non-Jews?	%	%

		Jewish	Non-Jewish
(29)	What percentage of the people in a neighborhood should be Jewish? Non-Jewish?	%	%

		Believe	Don't believe
(30)	What percentage of the adult Jewish population believe in God? Don't believe?	%	%

		Survive %	Not Survive %
(31)	What percentage of the non-Jewish community wants Israel to survive? Doesn't want Israel to survive?		

		Dislike Jews %	Like Jews %
(32)	What percentage of Americans dislike Jews Like Jews?		

		Belong %	Not belong %
(33)	What percentage of American Jews should belong to a synagogue? Should Not belong?		

		Attend Day School %	Not %
(34)	What percentage of American Jews should attend Hebrew Day Schools? Should not attend?		

Alternative Activities

There are many ways to utilize the "Percentage Questions" Activity. Here are some possibilities:

(1) Pick ten of the 34 questions and concentrate your efforts only on them, and then follow up by discussing one or two of them in small groups of three to five people and share and discuss your answers.

(2) Pick a number of the questions in this booklet and add some of your own. Discuss them in small groups of three to five.

(3) Select a group of questions revolving around one theme as a prelude to a debate, discussion, other format. Possible themes are: Jewish identity (assimilation, intermarriage, Americanism vs. Judaism, etc.); Observance of Jewish Law; Jewish Education; Jews as an American Ethnic Group; Prayer and the Synagogue; American Jewish Institutions; Jewish-Christian Relations, Israel as a Value for American Jews; Belief in God; etc., etc.)

(4) Ask participants to brainstorm a list of 25 new questions, similar in style and format to the ones in this booklet. Mimeograph them or read them aloud and ask participants to check their percentages. Then break into small groups to discuss.

(5) Whichever of the above methods are used, after the small group discussions, gather the groups together and follow up with a brief community discussion on: "I learned...", "I discovered...", etc. Such statements should be related to one's own life. This should then move into a discussion of any generalizations that grow out of the "I learned" statements of the entire group.

(6)   Finally, it's always good to end any values clarification activity
       with a discussion of "What next?" What ways can we apply what
       we learned to our own Jewish lives, to the Jewish community,
       etc. ? This "application" stage is very important if the activities
       and discussions are to have long-range effect and be more than
       "fun games."

                              ******

Sentence Completions

Goal

To explore some of our inner feelings towards ourselves, our friends, our life, our heritage. To share these feelings with friends, and to get to know each other better. People who know more about each other generally like each other more. People who know more about themselves are able to like themselves more too.

Instructions

Select ten of the sentences below which appeal to you most. After you complete the sentences, You will be asked to share some of the answers with the group. You need not share anything you choose not to. However, remember that the more you can comfortably share, the better people will get to know you.

Complete some of these sentences:

(1)   I feel proud when...

(2)   My favorite sport is...

(3)   I want my wedding to be....
        (or: My wedding was...)

(4)   Growing up in my synagogue was...

(5)   My Bar Mitzvah was...
        (I want my Bar Mitzvah to be...)

(6)   If I were in Israel right now I would...

(7)   I am most disappointed when...

(8)   If I had a million dollars...

(9)   Some holidays I like are...

(10)   My favorite day in Religious School was...

(11)   A beautiful teacher I had taught me that...

(12)   I am proud to be Jewish because...

(13)   I think a Jewish leader should be...

(14)   If I could make a tallis for someone in my family it would be....

(15)   I pray that my children grow up to be...

(16)   I wish the Chief Rabbi of Israel would...

(17)   The next time I study the Bible....

(18)   I wish God would...

(19)   What I love most about Shabbat is...

(20)   If I could pick any religion I wanted, I would..

(21)   Next Shabbat morning, I wish the rabbi would speak about...

(22)   If I had one wish for the Jewish people it would be that...

(23)   I am happiest when....

(24)   I think people should be more...

(25)   The meaning of the Shofar blowing on Rosh Hashanah to me is...

(26)   The ideal community for me is one in which...

(27)   If God were to make an announcement to the world tomorrow, I think it would be that...

(28)   The Jewish community in my city would be stronger if...

(29)   Some Jewish customs I'd like to change are...

(30)   I hope that...

                              ******

Follow-up Things To Do

(1)   Share some of the above completed sentences with the group. See how many of the group members shared similar thoughts. If someone reads a sentence that sounds like what you wrote, say so.

(2)   If any one or two themes were prevalent in the group, spend ten or fifteen minutes discussing that topic.

(3)   Discuss the topic: Why people don't share more of themselves unless asked to do so in a structured way.

(4)   Finish the following sentence in this activity book:

While writing the sentence completions I felt........

While sharing some of my sentence completions with the group, I felt......

While listening to others share their sentence completions, I felt.....

(This part of the exercise can be done in writing and then read aloud, or participants can just say aloud how they felt without writing it down first.)

(5)   To close this exercise, share some "I learned" or "I discovered" statements.

(6)   Alternative ending: Write down here, or share in the group, one or two things you'd like to change in your life as a result of the "Sentence Completion" exercise:

******

Jewish Values Whip

Goal

To help participants clarify in their minds what their views are to specific issues and problems in Jewish life. By giving each participant an equal chance to react to a question or issue, the members of the group stimulate each other with personal opinions and experiences. Each person has a chance to have "floor time" with no interruptions, a rare opportunity in many groups.

Instructions

The group leader takes one question at a time, reads it aloud, and then gives participants a few moments to reflect on the problem or issue. He then selects one person to give a brief and concise answer to the question (elaborating where necessary, but not at length). Continue around the room, in order of seating in the circle, with each person getting a chance to give his opinion, with no interruptions for other members. As with all values activities, anyone who wishes may pass.

Suggested Questions for Values Whip

1)   What is the most cogent argument for proving the existence of God?
2)   What Jewish book influenced you the most?
3)   How would you define "the good life" in one sentence? (Cf. Pirke Avot 2:1)
4)   What should the State of Israel be like twenty years from now?
5)   What should synagogues be doing about social injustice?
6)   What two Jewish sites would you like to visit?
7)   What would you do if the rabbi preached a sermon you disagreed with?
8)   What percentage of a person's income should go to Zedaka (charity)?
9)   What is an issue you believe in strongly?
10) What one thing would you like to change regarding the way American Jews observe Jewish mourning customs?
11) Do you want your wedding (your child's wedding) to be a big party or a small affair?
12) What would you like to happen to you after your death?
13) What does it mean to you to belong to the "chosen people?"
14) Why are some Jewish college students becoming followers of Hare Krishna, Zen Buddhism and other Eastern mystical sects?
15) What would you do if you were ushering in Temple, and a group of three students wanted to come in on Yom Kippur in "jeans"?
16) If a female Hazzan (Cantor) applied to your Temple, would you disqualify her for being a woman?
17) Name two things every Jew should do to observe the Shabbat?
18) Who is the best Jewish speaker you ever heard? Why did he/she impress you?
19) What is your view of a person who is religiously observant and takes advantage of his customers in business?
20) What kind of Jews do you want your children to be after you are gone?

21)   What is your favorite Jewish holiday and why?
22)   Name two ways in which Jews in America should be different from Americans of other faiths?
23)   How do you define "holiness?"
24)   What two "mitzvahs" would you like to perform next week?
25)   When should a person be "proud" and when "humble?"
26)   Is it ever permissible to fudge on the truth--to tell a half-truth? If so, Whe
27)   What values in Eastern European Jewish life would you like to restore?
28)   How should people make a "shiva" call?
29)   Should parents be required to pay Religious School tuition, or should all families pay equally (as in most public schools)?
30)   How can Yom Kippur be made more meaningful in your life?

Other Things To Do

1)   When one particular question becomes extremely controversial, open the discussion to the entire group after each member has had a chance to express himself once.

2)   Discuss: What did you learn about yourself or your group from the Jewish Values Whip?

3)   Write your own questions for a Jewish Values Whip in the space below:

       Now read it aloud and "whip" around the group, following the same procedur as before.

4)   Which questions were hardest for you to answer? Why?

5)   Invite a guest speaker to your next meeting to talk about a "hot" issue that came up in today's discussion.

6)   Ask participants to share any beliefs, attitudes or opinions they might have changed as a result of hearing the other members in their turn in the "whip".

7)   List two issues, problems or questions which you felt unprepared to discuss or comment upon intelligently as you would have liked.
       1)_____
       2)_____

What can you do to better inform yourself on this issue? List a few ways here:
       1)_____
       2)_____
       3)_____
       4)_____

******

Proud Whip

Goal

The Proud Whip is an extremely enjoyable and growth enhancing activity. It is short, simple and fun. It helps a person to appreciate himself, to recognize more of his own worth and to become more comfortable sharing his self-esteem with others. Participants also listen to things which make others proud, get to know them better as persons and stimulate their own imagination for future things they might do and be proud of.

Instructions

The facilitator "whips" around the room asking each participant to tell about something he did which made him proud. The choice of which item is picked will help the participant clarify what is important to him. Since not everyone is proud of everything, the right to "pass" should be exmpasized.

Each participant should begin with "I am proud that...." or "I am proud of...."

Sample Topics for Proud Whip

1) Something about Judaism that makes me proud to be a Jew
2) A Mitzvah (good deed) I did once
3) A time I served my synagogue
4) Something I did for Israel
5) A time I defended the Jewish People to a non-Jew
6) A time I suffered anti-Semitism and strengthened my Jewish identity because of it
7) A time I felt intensely Jewish
8) A speech I gave on a Jewish topic
9) Something I did to make my religion alive for me
10) A time I did something for elderly Jews
11) Something I did to help Soviet Jews
12) A new Jewish skill or area of knowledge I improved upon recently
13) A time I helped a friend celebrate a Brit Milah (cicumcision), Bar/Bat Mitzvah, wedding, etc.
14) Something I did to further Jewish education
15) A time when I acted with compassion
16) A time when I prevented an injustice from occurring
17) A time when I explained a Jewish holiday to a non-Jewish friend
18) A time when I did something special for my parents (children)
19) A time when I had a meaningful religious experience
20) A time when I forgave someone
21) A time when I was helpful to a mourner
22) A time when I visited a sick person and helped cheer him/her
23) A time when I was very hospitable
24) A time when I enjoyed reading a Jewish book
25) A time when I was very generous

Proud Whip

26) A time when I felt very close to God
27) A time when I helped my family observe Shabbat more meaningfully
28) A time when I was helpful to an animal
29) A time when I helped lead or arrange religious services
30) Something I did to bring honor to the name of the Jewish People
31) Something I did to protect a friend's reputation
32) A period or experience in my life when I learned a lot about being a Jew
33) A time I helped an Israeli or Russian Jew
34) Something I did to offer respect to a person (persons) of deep Jewish learning
35) Something I did for my grandparent (s)

Follow-up Things To Do

1) Think of your own topics for Proud Whip and go through the exercise
2) Discuss in full group: "How I feel when I talk about being Jewish."
3) Write here something which gave you great satisfaction in telling the group about yourself:

_____

_____

_____

4) Start a "Proud Diary" listing one or two things each day, or week which make you proud about yourself as a Jew and a human being
5) Share some "I learned...." or "I discovered..." statements in the full group
6) What things can you do in your "back home" life as a result of the proud whip? Share with the group
7) Write below what things you would like to do as a result of hearing others talk about pride in themselves:

a) _____

b) _____

c) _____

****

Values Focus Game

Goal

There are two important goals for this activity. One is to help people get to know each other better. Most small groups are composed of people who address themselves to issues of the weather, national politics, and other irrelevancies. Rarely do people reveal their true selves to others: their attitudes, beliefs, values on the crucial issues in their lives. The Values Focus Games presents a structured opportunity to share deeply in an I-Thou, or person-to-person way.

The other goal of the Values Focus Game is to train participants in the crucial skill of active, alert listening. No skill is more important in sharing oneself and in forming deep bonds of friendship than the ability to be fully present when another person is sharing deeply of his life, his feelings and values.

Instructions

Divide into groups of three.
In the space below, complete the following sentence:
I am most proud to be a Jew when _____

_____

_____

I am least proud to be a Jew when _____

_____

_____

Now follow this procedure: Each person will discuss with the group what he wrote on the above blank lines, taking five minutes apiece. One of the three in the triad should keep time. It is extremely important that while the "focus person" elaborates on his sentences, the other two participants give full and total attention to him.

There are three helpful ways in which the two active, alert listeners can increase the focus on the person sharing:

1)   Rivet your attention on the focus person. Keep eye contact with him while he is speaking. An occasional brief question is permissible if it does not change the focus away from the speaker.

2)   Be accepting and open. Be careful not to judge or criticize. Listen in a way that says: "It is possible that I may disagree with you, but I don't want to decide that until I have given you my full attention, heard your feelings and emotions, your values and attitudes, with empathy and understanding, getting into your own skin, as it were. I am not here to judge you, but rather to listen to you, to be with you, to be open to learning from you."

3)   Clarifying questions are permissible. An occasional question
which probes further into the speaker's feelings and attitudes is
permissible. However, be on guard not to ask things to satisfy
your curiosity, to gather information, or things which might shift
the focus away from the focus person. Also be sure not to reveal
negative feelings in your question.

Take time now to discuss these three rules: Why are they important, and
what results will they produce.

At this point proceed with the Values Focus Game. Each person speaks
for five minutes while the other two listen   actively, fully, alertly, intently
and emphathically.

*****

After each of the three people have had a chance to be the "focus person,"
you may take time to discuss, analyze and debate the positions taken on ideological
questions. Be careful to accept feelings - they are not arguable. Ideas can be
debated, but feelings cannot. See if you can distinguish between the two during
the discussion.

For example, if a person says that he feels proud when watching a 13-year
old chant a haftara, one cannot argue with that feeling. On an ideological, or
concept level, it is possible to argue that prayer is not meaningful, singing words
from the Bible is meaningless, or that Bar Mitzvah parties are too lavish. When
talking, stick to the issues, and still see if you can be accepting of each person's
feelings (that seeing a Bar Mitzvah chant a haftara makes him proud).

*****

At this point, discuss with your triad how it felt to have the full attention
of the other two members?

What lessons have you learned about communication? About sharing?
About relationships? Make some "I learned" statements about yourself. Try to
keep your learnings on a personal level, and do not turn it into a discussion of
educational principles. For example, one person might say: "I learned how
difficult it is to pay close rapt attention for five straight minutes without letting
my mind wander to tangential matters."

*****

Suggested Topics for Values Focus Game

My parents' observance of Judaism in our home made me.......
When I am drinking tea at an Oneg Shabbat or Kiddush I feel.....
If I could deliver one sermon in synagogue, the topic would be.....
The most important thing which my religion gave me is.....
When I hear about public schools or colleges holding important events on Jewish
holidays, I feel...
When I see Jews eat ham I feel....

Values Focus Game

If I were Chief Rabbi of World Jewry, a rule I would enforce would be.....
Something which Jewish People should do much more of is.....
A good way to keep children's interest in religion is.....
A time when I felt really good about being in synagogue was...
One of my favorite Jewish quotations is.....
Of all the Ten Commandments, to me the most important one is....
If I were stranded on a desert island and the only book with me were the Bible,
the book I would read most often would be.....
I feel most proud as a parent, when my children.....
The most exciting meeting of a Jewish organization which I ever attended was...
Being part of the worldwide Jewish People gives me feelings of...
When I hear people say Jews have too much money and power I feel...
If I had to pick one value I want my children to adopt more than any other it would be..
The most exciting teacher I ever had was...
When I am in a large group of strangers I feel...
If I were elected president of Hadassah of B'nai B'rith, the first thing I would
do is.....

******

Brainstorming

Goal

Widely used in industry, science and educational settings, brainstorming is a tried and true technique for generating a large number of possible solutions to a problem. The best brainstorming session is focused on a real, felt problem which a group faces right now. It elicits creativity and imagination from members of the group, who reach deep down into their sack of novel ideas to find new ways of solving old and new problems. Besides producing some wonderful, hitherto unnoticed possibilities for coping with our difficulties, it is a fun activity that generates a good deal of excitement and a flurry of noisy and useful activity in the group.

Instructions

In order for a brainstorming session to work properly, there are a few simple but important rules which must be followed:

1)   No criticism or judgment are permitted during the idea-generating stage. This tends to close down the process of creativity. If a person fears that his idea will be rejected, he will hesitate to put it on the table, and many a good idea has been lost that way. Remember this important rule: no criticism of any idea. It should be listed regardless of merit.

2)   Reach for bizarre and crazy ideas. The wilder the better! It's always easier to refine and tame down a crazy idea than to spark up a dull one. Often when reaching for the farthest and most unheard of possibility does a person generally come upon something new and unique. While some ideas produced this way may be absurd, one of them may just work. And, after all, it's only one we're ultimately looking for.

3)   The more ideas the better. We're looking for quantity not quality. It often helps to have two people writing the ideas down, each one taking every second idea. Otherwise, some good ones (or bad ones) might be missed. When a brainstorming session works well, the ideas often come flowing out like a gushing stream. Even if it sounds like one already suggested, or that it won't work, or that there are already to many silly, unworkable answers to a simple problem, suggest it anyway. The larger the number of ideas produced, the greater the likelihood that one of them may be that one precious solution we've been searching for.

4)   Piggy-back. Let another person's ideas suggest something to you. Build on others' ideas. Steal, plagerize, copy, whatever you have to do. When it comes to ideas, all is fair. One person's idea may be totally unworkable until a second person, hearing it, comes up with a slight adaptation which puts it into the winning column. Collaboration is the name of this game. No one takes author's credit for an idea in the brainstorming activity. Modifications, additions, subtractions, adaptations, combinations and permutations are all welcome.

Practice Brainstorming

Just to get into the swing of things, use this sample topic to loosen up your creative powers, unfreeze your imagination, and prime the pump of your innovative adrenalin (excusing all the mixed metaphors as you go, please).

Elect a secretary (not necessarily a female), who can write down the ideas (two is preferable, alternating) on a pad of paper, or better yet, on a piece of newsprint on the wall (or blackboard).

As soon as someone reads the topic, fire away, remembering the four
rules: 1)   no criticism of any ideas
          2)   the wilder the better
          3)   quantity rather than quality
          4)   Piggy-back, adapt, combine, etc.

Topic: You have enough melted wax to make ten Shabbat candles. Think of all the different simulated Jewish ritual objects you could shape out of this wax (assuming some minimal artistic ability to mold the wax). (Samples: etrog, challah, tefillin, mezuzah, kiddush cup, and, oh yes, Shabbat candles.) Do this practice session now!

Possible Ways to Shape Wax into Jewish Ritual Objects:

1) _____

2) _____

3) _____

4) _____

5) _____

6) _____

7) _____

8) _____

9) _____

10) _____

11) _____

12) _____

13) _____

14) _____

15) _____

16) _____

17)_____

18)_____

19)_____

20)_____

21)_____

22)_____

23)_____

24)_____

25)_____

Steps for Brainstorming Activity

Now you are ready to brainstorm in a more organizedly-chaotic way (you'll see what this means in a minute).

Step # 1:   Let each person take five minutes generating his own private list of solutions to a given problem.

Step # 2:   Form groups of three and generate from the private lists as many ideas as possible.   Take ten minutes for this.

Step # 3:   Let the whole group take another 15 minutes, acting as a committee of the whole, using the lists already created, to make as overflowing a bag of ideas as earthly possible.

Alternative Step # 3: Let each group of three then pick the three ideas they like best (now it is permissible to evaluate and criticize in order to arrive at group consensus on the best three ideas).   Then list each group's three ideas on a central board or sheet of newsprint.   A group discussion can then take place to find the best two or three ideas in the entire group.

Sample Topics for Brainstorming

1)   Your temple, club, Center, Federation, just formed a committee on social responsibility.   Think of as many ways as possible to help your organization get involved in making a contribution toward improving social conditions in our society, community, city, state, country or world.

2)   A neighbor of yours is about to have a baby and is desperately afraid that the child will grow up not appreciating his Jewish heritage.   How many ways can you think of to help inculcate a feeling of love and appreciation for Judaism during the first five years of the child's life (when, the psychiatrist tell us, all the important impressions and attitudes are really formed)?

3)   A group of twenty-five Soviet Jews have just settled in your community. They are having a difficult time adjusting to America and to American Jewish life.   Your club or organization has taken upon itself the responsibility of helping them feel more at home and happy living in your midst.   How many ways can you think of to do that?

4)   A local synagogue had a fire a short time ago, and has been renting
        temporary facilities in a motel. It is very uncomfortable there, and
        expensive, and they would like to raise the funds to rebuild their own
        structure as quickly as possible. How many ideas can you think of to
        raise the much-needed cash?

5)   Here's a light one. Your organization wants to change its name, Think
        of as many possible new names as you can.

6)   There has been a rash of sermons in neighborhood churches about the
        Middle East crisis, in which the minister or priest has taken an anti-
        Israel position. What techniques can be used to educate the local clergy
        group about Israel's position?

7)   What new courses could be offered next year in your local Hebrew High
        School?

8)   How many ways can you think of to make religious services more
        attractive to school-age children? To their parents?

9)   Here is a kiddush cup. Without talking, show as many funny ways as
        you can to use this cup.

10)   Make a very, very long list of programs which this group might use
        during the next five or ten meetings.

11)   List all the reasons why every Jew should support the State of Israel.

12)   Brainstorm a large quantity of ideas for strengthening Jewish family
        life in your community.

13)   List a lot of ways in which your group can help its members feel better
        about themselves.

14)   List as many ways as you can in which your organization can use Hebrew
        words in its administrative and organizational procedures.

15)   List as many people as you can who might be potential speakers for
        your organization during the coming 12 months.

Another possibility

        Brainstorm all the possible problems which your group faces which might
be solved through brainstorming. After finishing the list, pick the three most
important ones and brainstorm them at this meeting.

*****

Personal Coat-of-Arms

Goal

Psychologist Nathaniel Branden talks about four central concepts that help create a mentally healthy person: Self-awareness, self-acceptance, self-responsibility and self-assertiveness (The Disowned Self, p. 155). The Personal Coat-of-Arms will help a person get in touch with his own achievements, failures, strengths, weaknesses, goals, attitudes, beliefs, and self-concept. Practice exercises such as these help an individual come closer to Dr. Branden's four requirements for psychological well-being and personal effectiveness.

Instructions

In the appropriate position on the coat-of-arms shown on the following page, draw a picture, design or symbol of any kind which answers the questions that follow.

Do not concern yourself with esthetic productions or about the artistic merit of your symbol. Just draw what comes to mind. Do not use words unless specifically indicated (such as in a motto). Drawings can be as simple, foolish or bizarre as you wish. The only important thing is that it means something to you, not to anyone else. You will have a chance to explain its meaning to others, if you so choose, later.

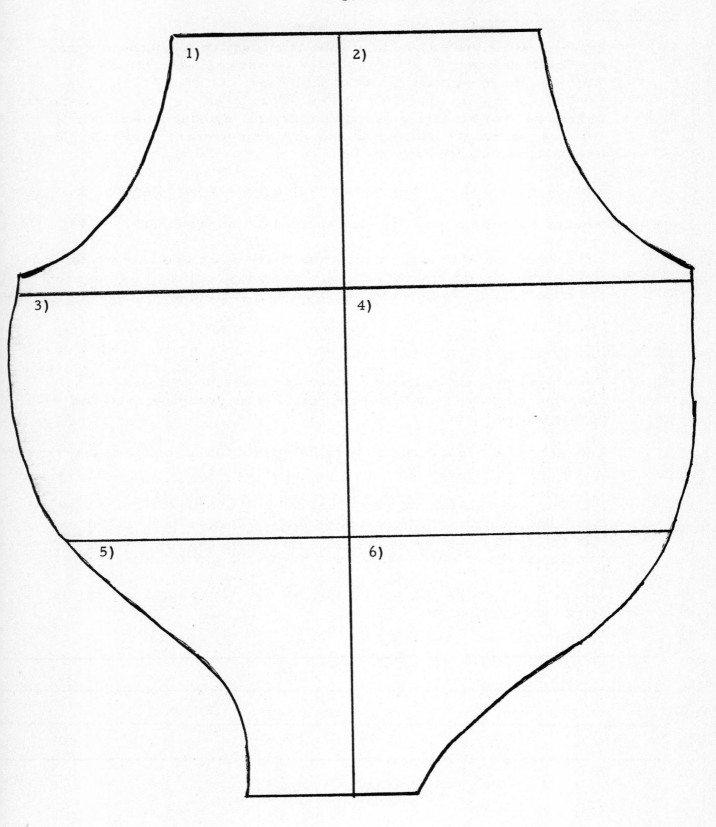

Personal Coat-of-Arms

Questions for Coat-of-Arms

1) In the area designated as #1, answer this question in a picture, symbol or design:
    What was the most exciting day of your life?

2) In area #2, answer this question in a picture, symbol or design:
    What was the most important thing about your primary family? (the one in which you grew up.)

3) What is something that others can do to make you very happy?

4) What is one area of your life that could stand improvement?

5) What would you wish if you were granted any one wish in the world?

6) Describe yourself in three words (here it is permissible to use words).

Other Things To Do

1) Form dyads and explain your coat-of-arms to your partner. Reverse, and have your partner explain his to you. Cover any box you don't want to share.

2) Let each person in a group of 10 to 15 explain two of the six boxes that he prefers to highlight.

3) Pin your coat-of-arms on your chest and mill around the room examining each other's signs and symbols. Then have the group take seats and make "I learned..." statements, sharing anything you discovered or were surprised at during the group milling.

4) List here two things you found out or re-discovered about yourself in doing the coat-of-arms:

(1) _____

_____

(2) _____

_____

JEWISH IDENTITY COAT-OF-ARMS

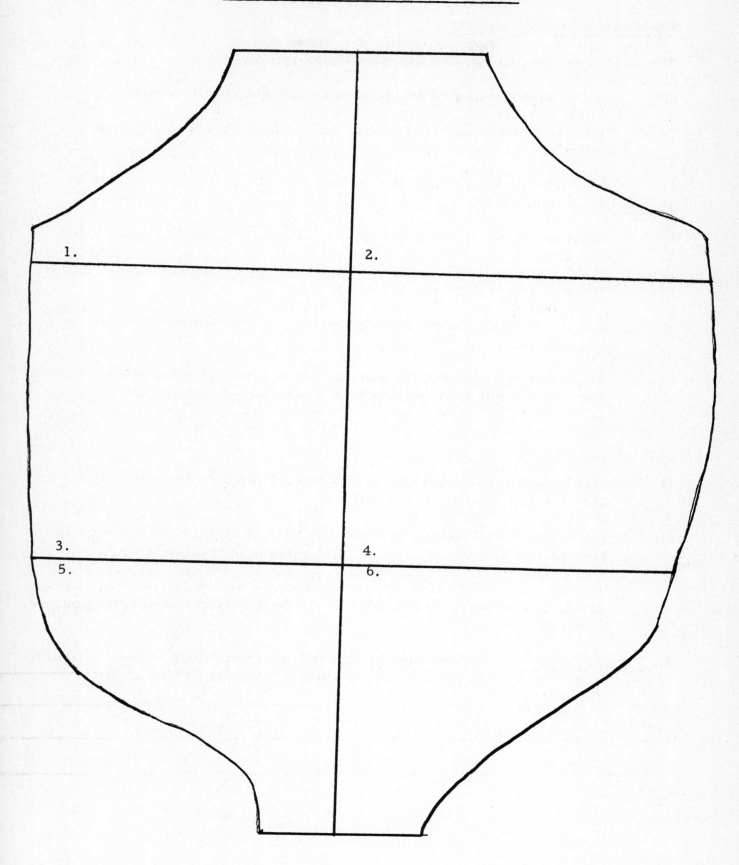

Personal Coat-of-Arms

Jewish Identity Coat-of-Arms

Now fill out the "Jewish Identity Coat-of-Arms".

1)   In the area designated as #1, answer this question in a picture, symbol or design:
What is some Jewish value you hold about which you would never budge?

2)   Describe the kind of Jew you would like to be in a picture, symbol or design.

3)   What contribution would you like to make to the Jewish People before you are 65?

4)   Draw a famous Jew with whom you identify.

5)   Draw a Jewish symbol or design which for you summarizes all of Judaism.

6)   Write two or three words, your own or a quotation from Jewish literature, which symbolizes your philosophy of Jewish life.

Other Things To Do

1)   Go through any or all of the four "Other Things To Do" that follow the first personal coat-of-arms.

2)   Were any Jewish values described in your first personal coat-of-arms? Compare the two.

3)   In what ways would your coat-of-arms have been different five years ago? In what ways do you think it will be different five years from now? Discuss in dyads.

4)   In groups of four, let each person talk about one thing he would like to work on in his life that emerged from making the Jewish Identity Coat-of-Arms.

Letters to the Editor

Goals

The object of this activity is to impress upon the participants the enormous power they have in the execution of the simple act of writing a letter. In our democratic society, public opinion carries tremendous weight - far more than the average citizen realizes.

It is ironic that the Letters to the Editor column in the daily newspaper is one of the cheapest and yet most effective means of communication and expression of opinion by the public at large. Surveys have shown that the Letters-to-the-editor section of the Editorial Page is one of the most widely and consistently read portions of an average newspaper.

As a minority group, Jews have a special duty and responsibility to keep the public alert with regard to issues that affect the Jewish people. This is not narrow parochialism, unless one blantantly suggests a course of action that is obviously detrimental to society at large in the hope of improving the lot of the Jews. The truth is that when society benefits, the Jews benefit, and vice versa. Thus, by taking the Jewish side of a controversial question, a Jewish person is, taking the side which is ultimately beneficial to all people.

Another major goal of this activity is to get people into the habit of writing to the newspaper (as well as to political leaders) often, even if the letter is not printed. Editorial policies often are strongly influenced by the views of readers as expressed in Letters to the Editor. Jews need to learn to use this inexpensive and effective tool more frequently and more effectively.

Of course, taking direct action, such as writing a Letter to the Editor, has a strong effect on the commitment of the writer toward his cause. It is a known principle in psychology and education that when one acts on a value, the value is strengthened as a value, helping the doer realize how much that value means to him. This pedagogic principle can be formulated in this simple phrase: expression increases impression. In other words, by expressing oneself on an issue, and by taking positive action regarding, one heightens the inner feeling and commitment, or impression, regarding that issue, raising it to the level of a value.

Instructions

1.   Each member of the group is instructed to write the editor of any newspaper or magazine in the country, and to mail it. He then brings a carbon copy to the next meeting of the group, perhaps as a ticket of admission to the meeting.

2.   The leader can ask the group members to organize themselves into groups, according to the themes of the letters. For example, all those who wrote a letter about Israel or the Middle East go into one corner of the room. (The leader might prepare in advance by hanging a sign at designated points in the room to help participants find their group). Those who wrote about Soviet Jewry into another corner. Other such groups might be: American politics; social action (ecology, racism, fair housing etc.); anti-semitism; family morals; etc. , etc. About six or seven broad categories should suffice.

Let those gathered together in one group share what particular sub-topics their letters focused on.

3.   The group at large (each person remaining in his small group) can then look around and compare the numbers in each category, and make some observations about that. Some possible explanations might be given (recent current events; a recent lecture on a certain theme; a controversial issue in a magazine or newspaper or T.V. show etc.)

4.   One representative from each group can then summarize some of the opinions, attitudes and feelings of his group. A general discussion can then follow, opening the floor to the entire assemblage.

Other Things To Do

Other possible follow-up strategies for the Letter-to-the-Editor Activity are:

1)   If and when members' letters are printed, xerox copies and send them in the mail (or distribute at a meeting) to all group members.

2)   Mimeograph a booklet containing all the letters written by the group and distribute to all members. As published letters are later mailed, members can insert them into the back of the mimeographed booklet, or, if blank spaces are left on every other page, right next to the mimeographed version. At the end of several months, the group should have a nice collection of mimeographed and printed statements of the strong view of their group members. This will make a lovely and meaningful souvenir from this group.

3)   Printed letters can be compared with the original ones, to study the process of editing done by the paper or magazine; what editors are looking for; what are effective ways of writing letters that will be printed (compare the letters that were accepted and those that were not, and analyze the differences).

4)   Examine the letter collection and see what issues are important to your group. You might find some clues for future courses, programs, speakers projects. etc.

5)   Prepare a flannel board or bulletin board of soft board material, and post all the carbon copies and printed letters at each meeting.

Letters to the Editor

6) At the end of the meeting during which letters were shared and discussed, ask each member to write another letter, stamp and mail on the way home. See what differences there were in the original letters and those written after listening to the ideas of the entire group.

7) Brainstorm ways of increasing the quantity of letters written by members of your group. (One such idea is to form a "telegraph bank" in which each group member commits himself to three public opinion telegrams a year (not more than $3 each), to be billed to his phone when a crisis emerges. This enables a group leader to send off several hundred telegrams immediately, bypassing cumbersome mechanical processes. This should not be a substitute, however, for individual responsibility of constant letter writing.

8) The same activity can be repeated several months later, or when an important community, national or international issue arises, with members being assigned to write a letter on a specific issue. The approaches and emphases of each letter can make for an interesting discussion and program.

9) Another version of the preceding suggestion is to have letters written to the President, or other public official, instead of to an editor of a newspaper or magazine.

10) Another possible activity can be picking the most interesting letter in the group, and have one member role-play the editor of the newspaper or magazine, debating the issue with the letter writer. Have the writer of the selected letter read it in person to the editor, and let the debate follow.

******

Jewish Values Voting

Goal

This exercise can be alot of fun, and a great stimulant for future discussion, learning and self-examination. It wakes up a group, gets the ball rolling, and is used often as an effective ice-breaker. Quick decisions have to be made, without too much prolonged cogitation and reflection, meaning that the answers come from the "gut" rather than from the head - often a more effective barometer of true attitudes. The exercise is also a good way to get people in a group to find out "who are the comers," - i.e., who makes up this group? What kind of people are here? What values do the people in this group hold? Is there a liberal or conservative tendency on certain important Jewish issues?

Often a group leader can return to some of the issues raised in Jewish values voting, at a later time in the group's life, and develop one or more of the issues into a full blown discussion or evening program. In this sense, one of the goals of the activity is to suggest future directions for programs, speakers, activities, and study sessions.

Usually there is a good deal of laughter during this activity, and that does provide a light introduction to some heavier things later. This does not mean, however, that some of the questions are not in themselves very weighty.

Instructions

The leader announces that the group will now do an exercise called "Jewish Values Voting, " as a way for people to get warmed up, and to begin to think and reflect on some important Jewish issues (perhaps related to a theme that will be dealt with in more depth later in the evening, or at another time). There will be five ways to respond to the questions the leader will ask the group:

Agree: raise hand
Strongly agree: wave hand
Disagree: thumb down
Strongly disagree: wave thumb
Pass: fold arms on chest

It is important to respond to each question with one of these five non-verbal responses; rather than just sit and not participate, perhaps thinking one does not have strong feelings on an issue. In that case the person could pass, or agree or disagree but not strongly.

It is important to let the group practice the responses before an actual question is asked. To practice, the leader tells the group that to get ready for this exercise, we're going to review the procedure. What do you do if you agree? (people then raise hands). What do you do if you agree

Jewish Values Voting

strongly? (people wave hands). What do you do if you disagree? (people put thumbs down). What do you do if you disagree strongly? (people wave thumbs). What do you do if you pass? (people fold arms on chest.

      O.K., Now we're ready. Leader then begins questions. Don't pause for questions or discussion or explanations. If a person wants clarification of a question, it is usually best to resist, but rather to let the person define the terms or clarify the best way he can. The purpose is for each person to answer the question he hears, not necessarily the one the leader has in mind. Sometimes a minor clarification is necessary, in which case the leader may respond to such a question.

      It is important for the leader to participate by voting on each question. However, it is best to vote a second or two after others, so they will not tend to follow the person at the front. Usually about 20 to 30 questions will suffice before people tire of this activity. On some occasions, even three to five questions can begin to motivate interest on a subject that will be dealt with in another exercise that follows Jewish Values Voting.

      Sample voting questions will be given below. The leader may make his own list, flowing out of his knowledge of the group and their background and interest, the theme of the program, or current issues facing the world and the Jewish community. At the end of the leader's questions, the group may be asked to shout out a few questions to the group. Some fascinating questions have come about in this way, and new insights about the askers and the respondants.

Sample Voting Questions

How many people:

- were born into a home that was Reform? Conservative?
  Orthodox? Reconstructionist? Secular? Zionist? Yiddishist?
- can read Hebrew
- keep a kosher home?
- have teenage children?
- have been to Israel? Three times or more?
- subscribe to COMMENTARY? SH'MA? MOMENT?
- think Israel should give up Jerusalem for a peace treaty?
- think Israel should give up the West Bank for a peace treaty?
- lit candles last Friday night?
- attend Shabbat services?
- would accept a woman rabbi
- would like women counted in the minyan?
- **would like women to have an aliyah at the Torah?**

Jewish Values Voting

- read Golda Meir's autobiography, MY LIFE?
- use seat belts?
- smoke on week days?
- think it's OK for a man and woman to live together if they are not married?
- think the religious school should teach sex education?
- would like more Hebrew in the Shabbat services? Less Hebrew?
- think they can relate to God in a meaningful way?
- think Jewish parents should forbid their children from inter-dating?
- live in the same city they were born in?
- would like one of your children to become a rabbi? a Hebrew teacher?
- think religion adds alot to life?
- have ever faced a serious crisis in life?
- think Jews are more assimilated today than 10 years ago?
- think affluence has adversely affected American Jews?
- think it is good for the Federal government to aid parochial schools?
- think marijuana should be decriminalized?
- think children watch too much TV?
- think Jewish kids are more spoiled than others?
- think Jews are more materialistic than others?
- think that temple board members should be required to attend Shabbat services?
- think too much of the American-Jewish charity dollar goes to Israel?
- think Hebrew teachers are underpaid?

******

Rank Orders

Goal

The rank order exercise will invariably produce critical and precise thinking on issues which have often been treated with sweeping generalities. The ranking, or prioritizing, of values, will press the participant to make subtle but important distinctions between two areas which are often similar but not identical. This fine distinction will help employ some of the critical thinking powers of people who have let their brains become dusty -particularly on Jewish issues. For others, it will give them a chance to reflect deeply on a question they probably have not had an opportunity to examine before in a more than cursory way.

Often participants will want to have several "ties" in their choices, rather than put one choice ahead of or behind another. This defeats the purpose of the rank order, and the person should be told that it is important to break all ties in doing this exercise. Even if it is difficult (especially if it is difficult), the choices should be made. By making these subtle distinctions, the participant will make new discoveries about his own value system. He will also realize that many decisions about Jewish living, and Jewish community action, take more careful thinking than previously thought.

Instructions

A series of choices are given, and the participant will be asked to prioritize these choices. This means, placing the numbers one, two or three (sometimes four) next to the choice in order of preference. Each choice must get a number, even if it is difficult.

Choices can be written on a chalk board, or handed out on a mimeographed sheet, or dictated orally asking participants to write the choices down on paper. After the three or four choices are given, participants take a few minutes to make their priorities, and can then share them.

There are several ways to do the next step, the sharing. Several random members can share their rank orders. Then a few others can explain one of their choices (highest, or lowest). Or, members can form small groups of 3 to 5, with each person explaining his rank order. There is no one right way to do the sharing, but some opportunity should be provided, in whatever way, for persons to exchange ideas on their priorities, values.

It is important to stress in this exercise, as in all value clarification activities, that there is no right answer on most questions. Given ten intelligent, informed, committed Jews in a room, their opinions on any given issue will vary widely. If there is an attitude of acceptance in the group, no one will feel put down because his viewpoint is not shared by others. Each person is entitled to his own views and attitudes. He should be asked only to listen openly to the opinions of others, and be ready to defend his own logic if asked, knowing that he has as much right to his views as others do theirs.

A climate of acceptance of all carefully considered opinions is crucial for this activity to succeed.

Sample Rank Order Questions

1)   To whom would you tell a deep dark secret?

_____   friend
_____   rabbi
_____   relative (spouse/parent)

2)   Which is worst?

_____   have an illegitimate child
_____   become dependent on hard drugs
_____   marry a non-Jew

3)   Where would you rather live?

_____   Jerusalem
_____   Eilat
_____   Golan Heights
_____   Tel Aviv

4)   Which would you rather study?

_____   Hebrew grammar
_____   American Jewish history
_____   Modern Zionism
_____   Bible

5)   Which biblical book is most meaningful to you?

_____   Psalms
_____   Esther (Megillah)
_____   Genesis
_____   Isaiah

6)   How would you prefer to spend a summer?

_____   at an archeological dig in Israel?
_____   Picking fruit on a kibbutz
_____   in a Mississippi ghetto
_____   counselor at a day camp

7)   Which would you rather be?

_____   Foreign Minister of Israel
_____   wealthly American Jew
_____   U. S. Senator

8)   What size synagogue would you rather belong to?

_____   over 1,000 families
_____   over   500 families
_____   over   200 families

9)   Do you prefer to worship:

_____   all in Hebrew
_____   all in English
_____   half and half

10)   Would you prefer your child to marry:

_____   a non-Jewish college graduate
_____   a Jewish auto mechanic
_____   a black Jewish physician

11)   Would you rather have a rabbi who is:

_____   a scholar and a poor speaker
_____   an average scholar who is great with children
_____   a great orator and involved in the community

12)   Which is most important before/during Passover?

_____   studying the Haggada
_____   eating matzah
_____   inviting the poor to the Seder
_____   marching for Soviet Jewry

13)   Which is most important?

_____   studying Torah
_____   doing good deeds
_____   regular prayer

14)   Which is most meaningful to you?

_____   listening to the Hazzan
_____   chanting prayers yourself
_____   silently reading the prayers

15)   If you had $1,000.00 to spend on, Jewish education, would you spend:

_____ $500 on teacher salary raises, rest on books and texts
_____ $600 on new audio-visual equipment, rest on texts
_____   entire sum on recruiting good staff

16)   Which is the worst problem facing Jews today:

_____   intermarriage
_____   assimilation thru secularization
_____   anti-Semitism

17) Which would you rather give your friend for a birthday:

_____   a trip to Israel
_____   an Israel Bond
_____   a trip abroad, half in Israel, half in Europe

18) If you had one hour to spend with the Prime Minister of Israel, would you:

_____   discuss US-Israel politics
_____   ask about his dreams for the Jewish people
_____   tell him what you think Israel should do

19) What is the most religious thing you could do:

_____   attend Shabbat morning services
_____   spend Friday night at home with your family
_____   read stories to orphan children

20) Which would you like to do most?

_____   learn more Hebrew
_____   become more active in the Jewish community
_____   become more ritually observant

21) If you had $500.00 to contribute to a Jewish library, would you buy books in the field of:

_____   poetry
_____   liturgy
_____   history
_____   philosophy

22) Which is most esthetically appealing to you:

_____   a menorah
_____   a Sefer Torah
_____   a Shofar

23) If you were stranded on a desert island, would you rather have with you:

_____   a Bible
_____   Siddur
_____   Talmud
_____   Shulchan Arukh

24) As a small child, which did you like best:

_____   Friday night dinners
_____   Passover Seder
_____   Hanukkah menorah lighting

******

Either-Or Forced Choice

Goal

This activity can be used as an ice-breaker, to warm people up to one another, at the beginning of a new group, or at the beginning of a program. It can also be effectively used at about half-time to energize the participants, since it involves a great deal of physical motion. Like the Jewish values voting activity, it will force participants to make quick intuitive choices, which they can then discuss at greater length, or expand into a full evening's discussion or program at a later time. It will stretch the imagination, and encourage some rapid choice-making on interesting issues.

Instructions

The leader asks group members to stand in the middle of the room. Chairs and other obstacles should be moved to the side. Participants will be given two choices, and they proceed to the side of the room indicated, depending on their choice. For example, the leader will point to one wall, or side of the room, and say, "Those who consider themselves liberal Jews go to this side," and then pointing to the opposite side, say, "Those who consider themselves traditional Jews go to this side. Members then go to the side they select, fairly rapidly. There they find a partner and each take a minute or so to explain why they made that choice rather than its opposite. Members then return to the middle, and are given a second choice, and find a new partner to share with. Each time a choice is made it is preferable to find a new partner rather than to keep exchanging ideas with the same person. About ten choices will suffice for one time. This is the kind of activity that can be used again and again at different meetings of the group, with changed choices. Sample choices are given below, but the group or group leader can make up many others.

Sample Either-Or Choices

1) more like Moses or Aaron?
2) more like Ben Gurion or Menahem Begin?
3) more American or Jewish?
4) more traditional or liberal?
5) more like Hillel or Shammai?
6) more like a Shabbat candle or a Havdalah candle?
7) more like a kippah or a tallit?
8) more like Freud or Maslow?
9) more like summer or winter?
10) more like Jerusalem or Tel Aviv?
11) more like a Sefer Torah or a printed book?
12) more like a synagogue or a classroom?
13) more intellectual or more emotional?
14) more ritual-oriented or more idea-oriented?
15) more like Shabbat or Yom Kippur?
16) more like an etrog or a lulav?
17) more Ashkenazi or Sephardi?
18) more like a home-baked Challah or a frozen kosher hotdog?
19) more like New York or San Diego?
20) more like a mezuzah or a kiddush cup?

21)   more like a scribe (sofer) or a priest (kohen)?
22)   more religious or observant?
23)   more positive or negative?
24)   more social or more private?
25)   more Hebraic or Judaic?
26)   more culturally Jewish or religiously Jewish?
27)   more like "Fiddler on the Roof" or "Good-bye Columbus"?
28)   more like Sammy Davis, Jr. or Elizabeth Taylor?
29)   more "bar" or "mitzvah"?
30)   more intense or dilettante?
31)   more El Al or Zim?
32)   more stable or innovative?
33)   more task-oriented or more person-oriented?
34)   more like Mt. Zion or Yad Va-shem?
35)   more like a friend or a parent?
36)   more monolithic or eclectic?
37)   more esthetic or more practical?
38)   more like science or literature?
39)   more like a synagogue or a Jewish Community Center?
40)   more like a Siddur or a Mahzor?
41)   more like Herzl or Ahad Ha'am?
42)   more like paper or parchment?
43)   more like the Shma or the Amidah?
44)   more like the Shulchan Arukh or the Jewish Catalog?
45)   more like a dove or a lion?

******

Jewish Values Continuum

Goal

This activity enables participants to feel a wide range of views and opinions on important issues rather than just one extreme or the other. It points up the importance of avoiding the "black or white syndrome." It also encourages them to take a public stand on their attitudes and values.

Instructions

An important issue is selected by the leader or the group, and two extreme positions on that issue are identified. A line is drawn on the chalkboard, or on newsprint on the wall, and each person is asked to come to the front of the room and mark his initials on the place on the continuum at which his views most nearly fall.

For example, the issue of allowing women to have an aliyah at the Torah. On the left extreme would be those who think women should have right at all times under any circumstances. On the right extreme would be those who feel that women must never be permitted to have an aliyah. To add fun and spice, the left extreme position can be marked "Feminist Fraydl" and the right extreme position "Shaytel Shayna". Between these two positions lie dozens of possibilities, from the person who thinks aliyot for women are OK only if not enough men are present to the person who says that a Bat Mitzvah girl can have a aliyah on the day of her Bat Mitzvah but never again, to the third person who thinks a woman can have a joint aliyah with a man but not by herself.

After each person, or a representative selection of persons if the group is too large, has marked his initials on the designated choice area, a discussion can follow. Usually the exchange of opinions and beliefs will be strong following the public commitment of a position.

Jewish Values Continuum can be used in several ways. For example, it can be introduced to expose a group to a new issue, which would be followed by lectures, reading, discussion to see if people make the same choices or not. Or, the activity can be used to wind up a study or discussion unit, as a way to tie things together and help people make action commitments.

A variation of the Continuum activity is to have a line across the floor, such as with masking tape, on which persons stand, according to the shades of their beliefs and opinions. The leader can see where small clusters of persons gather and ask them to summarize their position, and then a debate can take place between the clusters of persons.

Sample Questions for Jewish Values Continuum

1)   How much change should be made in ritual and liturgy?
"Judaism of the Heart" Harry . . . ."Torah from Sinai" Tommy

2)   Is it alright for Jews to seek out converts to Judaism?
Missionzing Marty . . . . You do your Thing Yussy

3)   Should children study Judaism in the English language or study Hebrew
     language and grammar to learn in the original?
English Ellen . . . . Purist Pesach

Jewish Values Continuum

4)   How do you conceive of God?
Rationalist Reuven . . . . Old-Man-in-the-Sky-Os

5)   How virulent do you see anti-Semitism in America today?
Paranoid Peretz . . . . Assimilated Adelain

6)   How can a modern Jew Observe the Shabbat?
26-hour Tilly . . . . As-much-as-you-can Al

7)   Are the Jews the Chosen People?
Exclusivist Exra . . . . Universalist Yetta

8)   Should marital partners be completely loyal?
Open Marriage Oscar . . . . Seventh Commandment S

9)   Is a Jew's major responsibility to social justice or Jewish survival?
Social action Shmuel . . . . Me First Menachem

10)   Is the Jewish home or the synagogue more important in America?
Friday Night at Home Freida . . . . President-of-the-schul-
                                                   Pinchas

11)   Is the purpose of Jewish education moral and spiritual development
       or Jewish identity?
Zionist Zeek . . . . Isaianic Ike

12)   Is American Jewry becoming stronger or weaker?
Bigger-and Better-Bertha . . . . Oy-Vay-Ofra

******

Public Interview

Goal

The Public Interview creates excitement, drama, and high interest in a group. It is one of my favorite strategies. It gives the person interviewed a chance to clarify and publicly affirm his stand on specific issues. It creates interest in the group, and motivates further discussion and exploration, individually or in the group. In addition, much factual learning often results from the Public Interview.

Instructions

Any member of the group can be interviewed by the leader on any subject. The leader may invite a specific person to be interviewed, or may ask for volunteers. Or, an outsider may be brought in to be interviewed, someone who is an expert on a particular subject of interest to the group. Each method has its time and place. When group members are interviewed, more of their own self is disclosed, and members get to know one another on a deeper level. Much learning about life takes place in this way.

The procedure is as follows: the person being interviewed goes to the front of the room (desk, podium, pulpit, etc.), and the leader, the one asking the questions, stands in the back of the room. The leader goes over the ground rules for the interview; 1) any question may be asked, 2) the person interviewed may always say, "I pass." 3) If he does answer, it must be honest, 4) the interviewee can ask the leader to answer any question he asks himself, 5) the interview can be terminated any time the interviewee wishes, merely by saying "Thank you for the interview."

As for subject matter, there are two possibilities. The subject of the interview can be completely open ended. That is any question about anything at all can be asked, personal, professional, academic, etc. A good variety between personal, value and attitude questions always makes for a spicey and interesting interview. The second possibility is that the interview revolve around one specific subject area: drugs, sex, religion, prayer, God, Bible, friendship, marriage, Israel, politics, American Jewry, etc.

If an outside expert is brought in, then the group will probably want to limit the interview to specific subject of the interviewee's area of expertese.

Another variation on the Public Interview is for a group member to role play a famous person, living or dead, and answer questions as if he were that famous person. Sometimes a group member can do advance research on the life and thought of such a person to be prepared to handle any questions that may come. (He can always pass).

Sample Interview Themes

1) Interview a Soviet Jew on Jewish life in Russia; on his experiences getting out of the USSR; or on his new life and how it compares to being behind the Iron Curtain.

2) Interview a person who just returned from a visit to Israel, Russia, or some other place of interest.

3) Interview a person who just went through an interesting experience: Mar Mitzvah, confirmation, wedding, being in a wedding party, having a close call with an accident, losing a loved one, seeing a famous person, reading a book, seeing a movie, etc.

4) Interview a person who has an interesting hobby: stamp collecting, history buff, model builder, autograph hound, etc.

5) Interview an older person about Jewish life as it was then, and how it compares with now.

6) Interview a person who is willing to share personal experiences: first date, converting to Judaism, attending a parent's re-marriage, being divorced, publishing a book, biking across Israel, being held hostage, being elected president of an organization, getting married, having a child, etc.

7) Interview a person who holds strong views on a controversial topic: Jewish women's rights; abortion; birth control; drugs and their legalization; Israel politics; improving Jewish education; Jewish community organizations and their lack of cooperation; liturgical reform, etc.

Sample Role-Play Interviews

Have someone play the role of a famous person, living or dead, and answer as though he were that person:

1) Moses having just received the Ten Commandments
2) Judah the Maccabee having just won Jewish Independence
3) Abraham having just been told of the coming birth of Isaac; or of going thru the Akedah.
4) Theodore Herzl after the First Zionist Congress
5) Ben Gurion at the Proclamation of the State of Israel
6) General Rabin after the Six Day War
7) The Prime Minister of Israel on the current situation
8) The President of the United States on US-Israel relations
9) An anti-Israel Arab on the West Bank
10) The Soviet Premier on Russian anti-Semitism

Public Interview

11) A Jewish poet (Yehudah Halevi) on the meaning of one of his poems
12) Sholom Aleicheim about the life of Tevye
13) A Soviet Jew who just arrived in Israel
14) The first woman rabbi
15) President Roosevelt on the Holocaust
16) A Holocaust survivor
17) Elie Wiesel on his childhood in the camps
18) A character from a novel
19) A controversial figure in the news
20) A recently deceased person talking from the next world

******

Group Interview

Goal

The group interview enables more persons to participate in the kind of "public interview" described in the last activity. In this case, several people can be interviewed simultaneously, and more people are involved, both answering and asking questions.

Instructions

The group is broken up into smaller units of five to ten persons. One interviewee is chosen, and the other members jot down questions to ask him. The interviewee might also write some questions and give them to people in the group - questions he would like to be asked.

The leader can assign topic, or each small group can select a topic, or the interviewee can select a topic. Themes should revolve around Jewish areas of interest, including beliefs, attitudes, values, practices, observances, commitments, current Jewish issues, controversial moral and social questions, or personal experiences.

The same rules apply here as to the Public Interview: the interviewee can always pass; he may return the same question to the asker; he must answer honestly when he does answer; and he may terminate the interview whenever he chooses by saying "Thank you for the interview." One additional rule in this activity is that the focus person calls on anyone he chooses to ask a question.

Sample Public Interview Topics

My Bar/Bat Mitzvah
A Recent Jewish Experience
My Belief in God
Things About Jewish Life I Like/Dislike
Some Rabbis I Have Known
A Pesach I Enjoyed
My Views on Abortion
My Views on Jewish Women's Rights
A Jewish Book I Recently Read
My Attitude Toward Christians
The Hanukkah-Christmas Dilemma
Federal Aid to Jewish Day Schools
My Views of Divine Revelation
Is The Bible Infallible?
My Ideal Synagogue
A Jewish Value I Hold Dearly
My Last Yom Kippur
Things I Have Done for Soviet Jewry
Things I Have Done for Israel
Things I Have Done for My Synagogue
Things I Have Done for My Local Jewish Community

Add your own Suggested Topics Here:

******

Conflict Dialog

Goal

The aim of this activity is to help a person get in touch with some of his inner feelings and attitudes about a specific conflict area. We each have several sub-personalities within us arguing for different things at different times. This exercise enables a person to see both sides of an issue, and to dialog over them in a way that both clarifies the issues and helps to come to a happy resolution.

Instructions

The leader explains to the group that we all have conflicting voices within us, taking different sides of an issue. For example, one issue the writer often thinks about is that of Hebrew Day Schools versus Afternoon Hebrew Schools. Should we put our energies into day school education, for the elite few, or concentrate more on afternoon schools for the masses of Jewish children? Of course both must be supported, but sometimes budgetary considerations make it necessary to allocate funds to one institution in greater proportions than the other. Which gets a higher priority?

The way this activity will help me is as follows: I would sit in front of the group on a chair, with a second, empty chair next to me, facing me. I begin expressing the point of view giving priority to Day Schools. Then I switch chairs and speak for my other side and answer my first opinion and argue in favor of Hebrew afternoon schools, and so on, back and forth, until some resolution seems to emerge.

Persons in the audience at this time may ask questions of either voice, both during and after the conversation. This may help the person clarify the issues even more. Another variation is to have the person write out a dialog between his two voices, and then come forward to act it out. This often helps to "prime the pump" and get the person into the issue more deeply and clearly. The acting out can then follow what was written down, plus carry it even further.

Another possibility is to have the group break up into smaller units of ten, and conduct several conflict dialogs at once. Each person doing the dialog can think of an area of conflict in his own life relating to some ritual, moral community or political issue. A general discussion can follow the conflict dialog.

Sample Conflict Dialogs

Should I Join a Conservative or Reform Temple?
Should I permit My Children to Interdate?
Am I Doing Enough for Soviet Jewry?
Should I Keep Kosher in My Home?
Should I Attend Services Friday Night or Shabbat Morning?
Should Israel Give Up Territory for Peace?
Am I Contributing Enough to Jewish Charities?

Add Your Own List of Conflict Dialogs Here:

******

Magic Box

Goal

   This activity will stimulate the imaginative faculty in the participants, and will encourage them to think about their goals, hopes, dreams aspirations. Often we limit our long-range expectations because we are told that it is not fashionable or healthly to fantasize. Fantasy is a tool that is becoming more widely used in education, and its use can be a powerful mechanism for expanding our options, encouraging our spiritus to soar toward newer, higher and better ways of being human and being Jewish. (See the writer's Jewish Consciousness Raising Handbook companion volume to this book, for more on fantasy exercises.)

Instructions

   The essence of this activity is that the leader asks a number of persons to imagine that they had a magic box in front of them. The box is labeled "Jewish." If they could have anything in the world for themselves or the Jewish community, or the Jewish people at large, what would it be? What would be contained in the box. The magic box can get larger or smaller, so size should not be a limitation. Furthermore, the box can contain something abstract or something very concrete. It can have a plane ticket to Israel, a renewed love relationship between a parent and a child, an agreement of trade between Syria and Israel, a fleet of Zim Line Ships, etc. The leader gives examples like these to the group to encourage the widest and broadest kind of imaginative thinking. Then the leader asks: What would be in your magic box - something which is Jewish, and which may be for yourself or any other person or group of persons.

   Sometimes people will respond with moral things, such as world peace. Any moral, social or individual value can be, and should be, included within the purview of something "Jewish." It need not be limited to some cultural, ritual or religious object or concept.

   There are several ways to carry out this activity:

1)   A group of five volunteers can be called up to the front of the room to talk of their "magic box" before the group.

2)   Everyone in the group can be asked to think of a magic box, and then five or six people can be called on to tell what is in their magic box.

3)   The large group can be broken into several smaller groups of five or six, and after each person decides what is in his box, each takes a turn sharing with his small group. (It is always OK to pass). Others can ask questions and discuss the contents after each person has a turn. Then one person from each small group can share what

Magic Box

is in his box before the entire large group. A general discussion can then follow.

In any case, persons should be encouraged to close their eyes and think quietly about what is in their box, before sharing with the others.

The leader may conclude by asking a few words about the usefulness of dreaming, hoping aspiring, of having "crazy dreams" which may never come true. All great ideas start off with a dream in someone's head, with their kind of "magic box".

******

Jewish Life Line

Goal

This activity helps participants get an overview of their Jewish auto-biography. By reviewing their past steps, they will have a better idea of what ingredients went into their present Jewish self, and what steps and experiences they might want to take next. It is usually a very pleasant experience to review highlights of one's past life, and the sharing of these experiences brings persons closer together. Besides the values of group cohesiveness, the benefit of getting perspective on one's Jewish life is usually very positive, and always helpful.

Instructions

The leader asks each participant to take a piece of 8 1/2 x 11 inch paper, with the long side horizontal. Each person draws a line across the bottom of the sheet. At the left side of the line the participant writes the date of his birth, and at the right side of the line today's date. Then, ten to fifteen highlights are written along the line, including approximate date and a word or two as a memory guide. A slash is drawn across the bottom line for each date.

Some dates may be: bris/naming, entering religious school, Bar/Bat Mitzvah, confirmation, a death in the family (funeral, etc.), graduation from Hebrew High School, a trip to Israel, marriage, an important lecture or discussion, a visit to an important person, a course in college, reading a significant book, etc. Each person's life line will be different. Any significant Jewish experiences can be included.

After each person has made his Jewish life line, small groups can be formed, and individuals can each share the parts of their life line they feel comfortable talking about. At the end of these small group sharing discussions, the leader can ask the groups to look for common themes, common problems, common highlights. Then each small group can talk together for a few minutes listing some of these, after which one person from each group can share these with the group.

At the end of this experience it might be useful to ask each participant to write down a few sentences about what they learned from the "Jewish Life Line" experience. These sentences can start with:

I learned that I...
I discovered that I...
I re-learned that I...
I was surprised that I...
I was pleased that...

Jewish Life Line

Then the leader can ask several individuals to share some of their "I learned" sentences.

The "Jewish Life Line" activity can be used effectively in conjunction with the "Epitaph" and "Who is a Jew" activities as a full program of an hour or more. Some group interviews around past Jewish experiences can then make an excellent two hour evening program.

******

Who Is A Jew?

Goal

This exercise helps the participants probe deeply into their minds and hearts to define for themselves their Jewishness. It never fails to produce fascinating results. It gives all present an opportunity to examine some of the major aspects of being Jewish, and see which seem to be most prominent in the minds of several individuals. What is mentioned in defining a Jew, and what is left out, both provide for interesting discussion and much learning.

Instructions

During a session dealing with Jewish identity, the leader will ask three participants to step outside. The first person is called back and the leader asks him: Who Is A Jew? After the person answers, the leader repeats the question, Who Is A Jew? (Or: What else is a Jew?). Each time, the leader keeps repeating the question. After about ten times, the leader will say, "Do you think you've given me all you can?" If the answer is no, ask it some more. When the person seems to have run out of answers, the leader says, "OK, you've given me alot of answers, you seem to have run out. Before you sit down, just give me three or four more." This will evoke a chuckle from the group, but it is serious. Though difficult for the volunteer, sometimes some of the deepest and most revealing and highest valued responses emerge at this point.

It is important to allow the person to stop any time he wishes, even though the leader is trying to make him go deeper through persistence. There is a delicate balance between "pushing" a person and forcing, pressuring and coercing a person. Pressure must never be used. A bit of friendly and gentle pushing, however, if done in the right spirit, can be very growthful and learningful.

After the first volunteer sits down, the second person is called in. The leader explains that he will ask him the same question as the first person, and that the reason for having him go out was so that his answers will be entirely his own. (This alleviates any fears of conspiracy, collusion, and hence anxiety). The leader then repeats the same procedure. Finally, the third person is called back, given the same explanation, and the same procedure.

At this point several paths are open to the group. One is for a general discussion to take place. Several people may want to comment on the common themes of the three volunteers, and some of the unique responses that one or two of them gave. Others may notice a particular definition of Jewishness absent from all three. Another person may comment upon the difference in the last few answers from the volunteers, after they seemingly had exhausted their store of definitions.

Who Is A Jew?

Another possible way to continue the activity is to have the group break up into small groups of four to six, and whip around the small groups with each person taking a turn to give one definition of "Who is a Jew?" After going around the groups six or eight times, a general discussion can take place.

Still another possibility is for all participants to make a list of as many synonyms of "Jew" as they can, and then have five or six volunteers read their lists.

At the end of this activity participants will have a far greater awareness of the wide variety of definitions of "Who is a Jew?"

***

Epitaph

Goal

The goal of this activity is to help participants take a long-range look at their lives, to encourage them to summarize their life goals and achievements in a concise and succinct way, and to enable them to establish closer recognition with their own strengths and contributions to their family, society, profession and/or community.

Instructions

The leader explains to the group what an epitaph is - namely, a brief description of a person's life etched on the stone marker erected by one's grave. Those who have been to a cemetery might have seen one, such as the following: Here lies William Fish, lover of humanity. Or: Herman Swerdlow, who raised the level of health care in his community.

Each person is asked to write a brief epitaph for his own life, preferably under twenty-five words. It is helpful if the leader writes his own first, and reads it, or writes it on the board. Here is mine:

DOV ELKINS

Searcher for a fuller, richer
more exciting and creative
life for himself and others

This activity can be processed in many of the same ways suggested for earlier activities. Namely, in small groups, or in the total group. This exercise in self-evaluation and self-introspection might lead to other values activities such as a self-contract, conflict dialog, public interview, etc.

******

I Urge Telegrams

Goal

This exercise enables participants to make a clear, concise statement about an important value in his life. It is an excellent device for heightening interest in areas of social change, and for encouraging commitments to value goals.

Instructions

The leader distributes a 4x6 card, or a Western Union telegram blank, and asks the group to think of an important political figure, in the United States, Israel, Europe, the USSR, the U. N. , or anywhere else, and to write a telegram to that person. The telegram should begin: "I urge you to...." The telegram can be limited to 15 words, or longer if sent as a nightletter.

Another way to use the "I urge telegrams" is for the leader to name a specific person and ask the group to send that person a telegram. For example, the local mayor, Governor, the President, State Legislators, Senators or Congresspersons, the Prime Minister of Israel, the Soviet Ambassador, a European government head, etc. These could relate to general problems, such as anti-Semitism, Israeli issues, or human rights in other areas; or to specific political and human rights issues of the day.

Participants can share their telegrams in small groups, or the leader can have five or six people read their telegrams to the whole group, or both.

In the classroom, or in an on-going group, members can save their telegrams, and after five or more are written during the year, the writer can look at them all and write some "I learned that I...." statements.

Some groups may decide to send their telegrams through Western Union, or to send a few representative, or composite, telegrams. (There is a special reduced rate for "Public Opinion Telegrams" and for "Night Letters").

"I Urge Telegrams" can be posted on bulletin boards, refrigerators at home or at work or in school, and a scrap book of them can be kept. They can lead to further projects carrying forward the ideas contained in them, and to further discussion on major issues of the day.

******

Something In Your Possession

Goal

Things we carry with us reveal alot about us, often without our even knowing it. When asked to pay closer attention to the objects we carry on our person, around our neck, in our wallet, etc., some fascinating things are revealed about our values, our experiences, our commitments.

Instructions

The leader explains to the group that we will now do an activity that will help us find out what we value, help us get to know each other better, and produce some interesting results.

The leader asks each person to take out three things from his wallet, purse, or on his person (around his neck, on his wrist, fingers, etc.). These should be three things which tell something about the person's Jewishness It could be a membership card, a photograph, a mezuzah around the neck, a pledge card or check for a Jewish charity, etc. (Several people selected their wedding ring; another person chose a Red Cross card indicating the date of blood donation, showing His Jewish value of commitment to the public welfare).

People will often come up with fascinating items. They are then asked to select one of these and share it in the large group, explaining the meaning and/or background of that object in terms of the person's Jewishness. Another alternative is to explain all three in smaller groups of 4 to 6 persons, and then each small group share some of their highlights with the group at large.

Another variation of this activity is as follows: Each person can take three things from his wallet, purse, from on his person, pocket, etc. One is something that is the most revealing thing with him. A second is the most valuable thing with him. A third is the most useful thing with him. These need not be Jewish things specifically, but often will be. An interesting aspect of the discussion that follows the explanation of the items selected is how many people chose Jewish things, and what did their selection reveal, if anything, about their Jewishness, and their Jewish values.

This activity can be used to help form small groups or committees within an organization which will be based on who is attracted to whom because of what three objects were selected.

******

Packing Your Bag

Goal

This activity helps participants assess the relative value of their material possessions and spiritual possessions.

Instructions

The leader explains to the group that we are going to pretend that we are going on a long trip to a new country, and live there for a long time. If we can bring with us only ten things which we now own, what would they be? (Excluding money).

Participants then write down the ten things they would bring, such as photo album, automobile, bicycle, paintings, jewelry, treasured pair of tefillin or other ritual object, a well-worn and sentimental kiddush cup, a favorite suit of clothes, etc.

For a group with strong Jewish loyalties and involved in Jewish life, it is not necessary to specify that the items be Jewishly related. Such Jewish objects will naturally be selected. However, with a group of pre-teens, or an adult group which is not Jewishly involved, it might be a good idea to say that at least three of the items taken must be related to one's being Jewish.

An alternative to listing the ten objects, it might be an interesting idea to have participants draw their ten things. This often produces a different kind of result. Or, draw yourself settled in your new environment with these ten things near you.

The exercise can be processed in the same ways as the earlier ones. The "I learned" statements would be especially useful after this activity.

******

The Self Contract

Goal

The Self Contract helps bridge the gap between ideals and practice, goals and their implementation. Often in personal growth and value clarification activities participants deal with abstractions and nebulous ideas. The Self Contract is an excellent exercise with which to conclude a group meeting because it pins down the next step in carrying out the values discussed. In Jewish tradition, the best kind of study is that which leads to good deeds.

Instructions

The leader explains that a good way to conclude an exercise, a program, or a study unit, is to make some positive commitment to action. We do this with a Self Contract. This is not a contract with any authority figure, a rabbi, a teacher, or a parent. It is an agreement, a covenant, with oneself. A promise to change something about our life. Something we want to learn. Something we want to do more of, or less of, or do differently.

A Self Contract can be made, for example, to stop gossiping, or to learn to read Hebrew, or to learn a new song, or to save money to go to Israel, or to read three Jewish books this year, or to begin reading portions of the Bible weekly, or to write a letter every month to a Soviet Jew.

The Self Contract is written, and should be witnessed by another member of the group. There should also be a reminder date, a "check-up" point, so that the witness can see how far along the person is in achieving the goal. This does not mean that the commitment is made to the witness. The witness is merely a person who helps us bring out the best in and to ourselves. He is a helper, rather than a watchman or enforcer.

A good contract should have a completion date so that it will be easier to judge if the contract to oneself is truly fulfilled. Finally, a useful contract to oneself, to make important changes in one's life, should be concluded with some kind of celebration, party, or "burning of the contract" ceremony.

(For use of the Self Contract for Bar/Bat Mitzvah children, see the writer's Humanizing Jewish Life: Judaism and the Human Potential Movement, page 143).

     The leader is wise to remind the makers of the Self Contract not to make promises that are unrealistic and beyond their scope to fulfill. On the other hand, it should be difficult enough to require effort and commitment.

     After Self Contracts are written, witnessed, and all the details such as reminder date, completion date, means of celebration, are filled in, several persons can read theirs to the group.

Sample Self Contract

Today's Date _____

I, _____, because I want to

_____, promise myself that I will

_____

_____   _____
Signature of contract maker   signature of witness

Completion date_____   Reminder date_____

Means of Celebration_____

******

EXPERIENCE # 1:   RANK ORDERS

Goals:

1) Clarification of values and attitudes toward key issues facing Jewish leadership

2) Getting acquainted - finding out about the ideas and feelings of other members in the group

3) Promote lively discussion on important Jewish issues of the day

4) Relate some of the key questions of Jewish leadership development to the personal interests and desires of participants. This encourages discussants to take a closer look at their own relationship to world Jewry and its current problems and needs

Time Required: 30 minutes

Steps:

1) Facilitator explains goals of exercise, emphasizing that "rank orders" is a device being used in modern education to help people give priorities to their values, attitudes and feelings. In this case, the issues dealt with relate to current Jewish problems and challenges to Jewish leadership.

2) Form sub-groups of five or six. These groups can remain for the balance of the program to foster closeness, comfort and mutual understanding.

3) Each person chooses three of the six sets on the rank orders sheet and fills in each blank line with a number, so that within each set every choice is given a priority ranking. It is important that the facilitator point out at this point that there are no "right answers". All opinions are personal and therefore valid for that individual.

4) Each person is asked to share one or more rank orders with his/her sub-group, and to explain how and why these specific choices and rankings were decided upon.

5) After sufficient time has passed to enable each person to share one rank order (this can be checked by asking two or three small groups if they have finished sharing one rank order per member) everyone in the room is asked to reflect upon the experience: doing the ranking individually, sharing one set of priorities, and hearing the positions of others. Each participant is then asked to complete positions of others. Each participant is then asked to complete this sentence: Something I learned during this rank order exercise is. . Facilitator then calls on 4 or 5 persons in the large group - perhaps one from each small group - to share their "Something I learned. ." sentence.

RANK ORDERS FOR JEWISH LEADERSHIP DEVELOPMENT PROGRAM

1. If you were a Jewish communal worker, would you be a:

    _____ teacher in a Jewish School
    _____ director of Federation Planning Department
    _____ director of JCC athletic and health program
    _____ specialist in a CRC (Jewish Community Relations Council)

2. To which would you give lowest priority today:

    _____ fighting anti-Semitism in the U.S.
    _____ Jewish day schools
    _____ Soviet Jewry
    _____ local old-age home

3. Which is the most important quality for a Jewish leader?

    _____ observance of Jewish traditions
    _____ financial generosity
    _____ being articulate and persuasive
    _____ sense of humor
    _____ possesses a philosophy of Jewish life

4. Which course would be most helpful to a Jewish lay leader?

    _____ Comtemporary Middle Eastern Affairs
    _____ Ethics of the Talmud
    _____ Modern Jewish Philosophy
    _____ Human Relations Skills
    _____ History and Sociology of the American Jewish Community

5. Would you rather:

    _____ address a gathering of Jews in Madison Square Garden
    _____ take part as a paratrooper in the Entebbe raid
    _____ become president of CJFWF (Council of Jewish Federations
                     and Welfare Funds)
    _____ write a book about American Jewry

EXPERIENCE # 2   JEWISH LIFE LINE

Goals:

    1)   Community building

    2)   Self-examination regarding Jewish development

    3)   Motivation for further development and direction

Time Required: 30 minutes

Steps:

    1)   Take pen and paper and draw a straight line across the bottom
          the page.

    2)   The far left is the date of your birth. The far right is today.
          In between mark the approximate dates of significant events in
          your development as a Jew, beginning with your earliest memories.
          Such important turning points might be: your first day in religious
          school; your bar/bat mitzvah; a meeting with your rabbi or
          teacher; a trip to Israel; the death of a loved one; your election to
          community office, etc. etc. (10 minutes)

    3)   Discuss in small groups (five or six), Each person shows his
          life line and points out two or three highlights (10 minutes).

    4)   Group may look for common themes, experiences (5 minutes).

    5)   One person in each group summarizes highlights for the entire group.

EXPERIENCE # 3   JEWISH LEADERSHIP
REACTION SHEETS

Goals:

1)   To heighten awareness of major Jewish issues

2)   To express attitudes, feelings and personal values regarding Jewish issues

Time Required: 25 minutes

Steps:

1)   Facilitator passes out Jewish leadership Reaction Sheets to each participant.

2)   Each person individually fills in two sentences after each quotation: (a) a personal reaction; and (b) an application to Jewish community work/role. (10 minutes)

3)   Each person circles one number on the sheet that is next to the quotation which elicited the strongest personal feelings from him.

4)   Each person shares in groups of five or six which quotation he circled and why he selected that one, as well as the two sentences he wrote after it. (10 minutes)

5)   One person from each small group shares the quotation he/she selected and states in a brief sentence why he selected it and the application he sees it has to current Jewish Community life.

to be reproduced for distrubution to participants

JEWISH LEADERSHIP REACTION SHEETS

Instruction: After each quotation, write one sentence giving your personal feelings, attitudes, about the statement; then write a second sentence describing how this statement applied to your work in the Jewish community.

1) "The synagogue must be recognized as the primary instutution of Jewish life."
RABBI MAX ARZT
Jewish Theological Seminary

Personal reaction:

Jewish community:

2) "The Jews of America cannot live without English but will not survive without Hebrew."
SOLOMON SCHECHTER

Personal reaction:

Jewish comminity:

3) "He who sustains God's creatures is as though he had created them."
MIDRASH TANCHUMA

Personal reaction:

Jewish community:

4) "A person should so live that at the close of every day he can repeat: I have not wasted my day."
ZOHAR

Personal reaction:

Jewish community:

5) "Our quarrel is not with Jews who are different but with Jews who are indifferent."
RABBI STEPHEN S. WISE

Personal reaction:

Jewish community:

6) "The Jewish Federations of North America represent a fusion of fundamental Jewish purposes and principles with the American environment and society."
PHILIP BERNSTEIN

Personal reaction:

Jewish community:

EXPERIENCE # 4   LISTENING TRIOS

Goals:

1) To build listening skills

2) To achieve closeness among group members

3) To improve quality of interpersonal relationships among task groups

4) To give participants an opportunity to articulate on key Jewish issues

Time Required: 45 minutes

Steps:

1) Facilitator explains goals of the activity.

2) Trios are organized.

3) Participants decide who will be A, B, C.

4) Facilitator gives instructions:

    A is first speaker, choosing own topic from list.
    B is first listener; C is first observer.
    Speaker talks for five minutes.
    Listener summarizes for two minutes.
    Speaker and/or observer make certain listener does not omit,
     distort, add to, or interpret what speaker has said.
    Rotate roles so that each person plays each role

5) Begin Round 1. Facilitator stops group after seven minutes and
answers procedural questions.

6) Round 2: B is speaker, C is listener, A observer. New speaker
chooses own topic. Same time frames.

7) Round 3: C is speaker, A listener, B observer.

8) Participants in each trio discuss what they learned in terms of
listening skills

9) Entire group share generalizations about the communication process.

10) Applications to Back Home - local community, Federation, etc.

NOTE: to be reproduced for distribution to participants

TOPICS TO CHOOSE FROM (EXPERIENCE #4)

The Importance of Ritual in Judaism

A Good Jewish Book I read Recently

All Jews Are Responsible One For Another

Combatting Apathy and Assimilation

The Trouble with Jewish Organizations

Should We Criticize Israel Publicly?

Which should we fight for Soviet Jewry:
  freedom to leave or to live as Jews in the USSR?

Federation-Synagogue Relationships

Ways to Improve Jewish Education

Should Federations Support Congregationsl Schools?

Federation's Role in Social Action (gun control,
  hunger, pollution, affirmative action, detente)

Creating A Jewish Home

SUMMARY AND EVALUATION

Goals:

1) To tie together the loose pieces of the workship experience

2) To give participants an opportunity to focus and nail down their learnings, and consider applications to their local community situation

3) To assure the understanding is conveyed that this is a serious educational design, and has considered value for personal and Jewish growth as well as for enjoyment and creating a warm atmosphere.

Time Required: 15 minutes

Steps:

1) Each person writes down completions to any or all of the following sentence stubs. Sentences should be ketp short and to the point. Facilitator should give one or two examples first.

I learned...

I re-learned...

I discovered...

I re-discovered...

I noticed that...

I was pleased that ..

I was surprised that..   (5 minutes)

2) Facilitator asks volunteers to read one of their sentences to the total group, prefacing this by assuring the group that there are no "right" answers. To assure the free flow of this evaluation, no discussion of sentences is permitted; this might tend to reduce the mood and intensity of this activity.   (5 minutes)

3) Facilitator summarizes and concludes workshop, mentioning some or all of the following:

a)   highlights of some of the learning mentioned in the
      sentences just read ("I learned....")

b)   points out the special features of this Values Clarification
      approach: It draws on feelings and attitudes as well as facts
      and information; it is experiential, involving participants
      activity in the learning process through small group
      participation; and the learning comes from other participants
      rather than from some "expert" at the front of the room.

c)   The sense of warmth and fellowship that develops in this
      educational modality is perhaps one of its major gains.
      Participants get to know one another on a level that is far
      deeper than the usual cocktail party conversation. It is the
      truest and highest meaning of the Hebrew phrases "Havurah"
      or Judaic fellowship. Philosopher Martin Buber described
      such human dialogue, in which interlocutors-share themselves
      in the most profound sense, a meeting of "I-Thou."

The Hasidic sage, the Maggid of Kozhenitz, articulated the transcendent
spiritual and Jewish dimension of such community in the following words:

"Man aspiring to heights must reach for them through others,
with their help and helping them. If all of Israel's children
joined hands, they would form a chain and touch the celestial throne."

******

EXPERIENTIAL LEARNING

Dr. Dov Peretz Elkins is a pioneer in the field of religious education and human development. He combines the wisdom, experience, training and insight of the talmudic sage and the modern behavioral scientist.

He has produced a series of important and valuable volumes on a new, exciting, challenging, and growth-producing way to learn. To learn about religion, the Jewish People, about yourself, about how to establish meaningful relationships, how to strengthen Jewish family life, and about the art/science of mench-ology (how to become a "mench" - a self-actualizing, fully-mature, fully functioning human being).

Dr. Elkins

Finally, A New, Exciting And Enjoyable Way To Learn

Send order form below to: Growth Associates, Human Relations Consultants and Publishers, Box 8429, Rochester, NY 14618, 716/244-1225.